Crowdfunding for Environmental Sustainability and the Circular Economy

Filippo Corsini · Marco Frey

Crowdfunding for Environmental Sustainability and the Circular Economy

Empowered Strategies for Sustainable Growth

Filippo Corsini
Scuola Superiore Sant'Anna
Pisa, Italy

Marco Frey
Scuola Superiore Sant'Anna
Pisa, Italy

ISBN 978-3-031-66210-2   ISBN 978-3-031-66211-9   (eBook)
https://doi.org/10.1007/978-3-031-66211-9

© The Editor(s) (if applicable) and The Author(s), under exclusive license to Springer Nature Switzerland AG 2024

This work is subject to copyright. All rights are solely and exclusively licensed by the Publisher, whether the whole or part of the material is concerned, specifically the rights of translation, reprinting, reuse of illustrations, recitation, broadcasting, reproduction on microfilms or in any other physical way, and transmission or information storage and retrieval, electronic adaptation, computer software, or by similar or dissimilar methodology now known or hereafter developed.
The use of general descriptive names, registered names, trademarks, service marks, etc. in this publication does not imply, even in the absence of a specific statement, that such names are exempt from the relevant protective laws and regulations and therefore free for general use.
The publisher, the authors and the editors are safe to assume that the advice and information in this book are believed to be true and accurate at the date of publication. Neither the publisher nor the authors or the editors give a warranty, expressed or implied, with respect to the material contained herein or for any errors or omissions that may have been made. The publisher remains neutral with regard to jurisdictional claims in published maps and institutional affiliations.

Cover illustration: © Melisa Hasan

This Palgrave Macmillan imprint is published by the registered company Springer Nature Switzerland AG
The registered company address is: Gewerbestrasse 11, 6330 Cham, Switzerland

If disposing of this product, please recycle the paper.

CONTENTS

1 Introduction — 1
  1.1 Sustainability and the Circular Economy — 2
  1.2 The Role of Corporations and Enabling Factors for the Transition — 5
  1.3 Volume Structure — 8
  References — 9

2 The Paradigm of the Circular Economy: Barriers and Enabling Factors for Companies — 13
  2.1 The Need for a New Production and Consumption Paradigm — 14
  2.2 The Paradigm of Circular Economy — 15
  2.3 Circular Economy in European Policies — 22
  2.4 Barriers to Circularity — 24
  2.5 How to Finance the Transition? — 29
  2.6 Crowdfunding as an Enabling Tool for Circular Transition in Companies — 31
  References — 33

3 Funding the Future of the Planet Through Crowdfunding — 37
  3.1 The Origins of Crowdfunding — 38
  3.2 Anatomy and Operation of Crowdfunding — 41
  Subjects Initiating a Crowdfunding Project — 41
  Crowdfunding Platforms — 43

	The Financiers of a Crowdfunding Campaign	46
3.3	*Types of Crowdfunding and Examples of Circularity Campaigns*	48
	Donation-Based Crowdfunding	49
	Reward-Based Crowdfunding	49
	Loan-Based Crowdfunding	51
	Equity Crowdfunding	54
3.4	*Specialization in Crowdfunding Platforms for the Environment*	56
	References	57

4 Crowdfunding and Design for Circularity: The State of the Art and Relevant Examples — 61

4.1	*The Concept of Design for Circularity*	62
	Products Made with Circular Materials	63
	Long-Lasting Products	66
	Efficient Use Products	67
	Products Designed for End-of-Life Management	68
	Further Approaches to Circular Design	69
4.2	*Insights on Circular Products Developed Through Crowdfunding Platforms*	70
4.3	*Examples of Crowdfunding Projects for the Development of Circular Products*	74
4.4	*A Deeper Investigation of the Projects for the Development of Circular Products*	75
4.5	*Conclusions*	77
	References	78

5 Success Factors in Sustainability and Circularity-Oriented Crowdfunding Campaigns — 81

5.1	*Success Factors in Crowdfunding*	82
	Success Factors in Donation-Based Crowdfunding	82
	Success Factors in Reward-Based Crowdfunding	84
	Success Factors in Equity Crowdfunding	85

	Success Factors in Lending Crowdfunding	86
5.2	*Do the Sustainability and Circularity Features of a Crowdfunding Project Impact the Likelihood of the Initiative's Success?*	87
5.3	*Factors of Success Discussed in Literature on Crowdfunding Campaigns Focused on Sustainability and Circularity*	91
	Factors of Success Analyzed in Literature: Theoretical Frameworks Motivating the Research	91
5.4	*Analysis of Variables Pertaining to the Crowdfunding Campaign*	103
	Variables Associated with the Crowdfunding Campaign as Success Factors	103
	Variables Associated with Financiers as Success Factors	105
	Variables Related to Communication in Crowdfunding Campaigns	105
	Variables Related to the Sustainability and/ or Circularity Dimensions of the Project	106
	Variables Pertaining to the Proponent or the Proposing Team	107
	Variables Related to the Description and Presentation of the Project	109
	Variables Pertaining to the Reference Market	110
	Variables Related to the Perceived Quality and Progress of the Project	112
5.5	*Conclusions*	112
	References	113

6 Crowdfunding, Fraudfunding, and Greenwashing — 119

6.1	*Fraud in Crowdfunding: A Taxonomy of Fraudfunding*	120
	Frauds in Donation-Based Crowdfunding	121
	Perceived Frauds and Performance Issues in Reward-Based Crowdfunding	122
	Frauds in Loan-Based Crowdfunding	123
	Frauds in Equity Crowdfunding	125

viii CONTENTS

6.2	*Greenwashing as a Form of Fraud*	126
	How Is Greenwashing Manifested?	129
6.3	*The Dimension of Greenwashing in Reward-Based Campaigns*	131
6.4	*How to Discourage Fraud and Greenwashing in Crowdfunding*	136
References		138

7 Crowdfunding and Proactive Environmental Strategies in the Organizational Life Cycle — 141

7.1	*Crowdfunding in the Organizational Life Cycle*	142
7.2	*Proactive Environmental Strategies in Organizational Life Cycle*	144
7.3	*Questionnaire for Businesses that Have Conducted a Reward-Based Crowdfunding Campaign to Develop a Circular Product*	146
7.4	*Comparison Among Companies that Have Utilized Crowdfunding in the Phases of Birth, Growth, and Maturity to Develop a Circular Product*	149
7.5	*Environmental Certifications as a Sustainability Strategy*	152
	Certified Environmental Management System (ISO 14001 and EMAS)	156
	The B-Corp Certification	157
	Product Certifications	158
	Interest in Environmental Certifications Among Companies that Have Conducted a Crowdfunding Campaign	159
7.6	*Conclusions*	160
References		162

8 Conclusions — 163

8.1	*Crowdfunding as an Enabler of Prosumerism*	163
8.2	*Crowdfunding as a Tool for Initiating New Circular Business Models*	166
8.3	*Managerial Considerations for Conducting a Crowdfunding Campaign for Sustainability Projects*	167

CONTENTS   ix

*8.4   Role and Strategies of Platforms Specializing
in Supporting Projects Generating Positive
Environmental Impact*   168
References   169

Index   171

List of Figures

Fig. 2.1	Extraction of raw materials from the biosphere (*Source* Adapted from The World Bank, 2022)	14
Fig. 2.2	First schematic representation of a circular economic system (*Source* Adapted from Stahel, 1982)	17
Fig. 3.1	Relationship between stakeholders in the crowdfunding process (*Source* Adapted from Haas et al., 2014)	42
Fig. 3.2	Risk-reward relationship in relation to reward types (*Source* Adapted from Hemer et al., 2011)	45
Fig. 3.3	Types of crowdfunding (*Source* Authors' elaboration)	48
Fig. 4.1	Lock-in of a product's environmental impacts in relation to its life cycle phases (*Source* Adapted from Handfield et al., 2001)	63
Fig. 4.2	Trends of projects for the development of circular products over time (*Source* Authors' elaboration)	72
Fig. 4.3	Distribution of projects for the development of circular products by proponents' origin (*Source* Authors' elaboration)	72
Fig. 4.4	Distribution of projects for the development of circular products by type of circular product (*Source* Authors' elaboration)	73
Fig. 5.1	Trend in research on success factors in crowdfunding campaigns over time (*Source* Authors' elaboration)	83
Fig. 6.1	Default rates reported by commercial banks (2023) (*Source* Authors' elaboration based on Federal Reserve data)	124

xii LIST OF FIGURES

Fig. 6.2 Licensing status of equity crowdfunding platforms (*Source* Adapted from Ziegler et al., 2021) 126

Fig. 6.3 Perception of the greenwashing phenomenon (*Source* Authors' elaboration) 134

Fig. 6.4 Perception of greenwashing on major reward-based crowdfunding platforms (*Source* Authors' elaboration) 135

Fig. 6.5 The role of platforms in limiting the phenomenon of greenwashing (*Source* Authors' elaboration) 136

Fig. 7.1 Organizational life cycle (*Source* Adapted from Barringer & Ireland, 2010) 143

Fig. 7.2 Circular initiatives undertaken by newly established companies after the crowdfunding campaign (inception stage) (*Source* Authors' elaboration) 149

Fig. 7.3 Circular initiatives undertaken by companies in the growth phase (*Source* Authors' elaboration) 150

Fig. 7.4 Circular initiatives undertaken by companies in the maturity phase (*Source* Authors' elaboration) 151

Fig. 7.5 Interest in certifications among companies promoting a crowdfunding campaign for the development of a sustainable product (*Source* Authors' elaboration) 160

LIST OF TABLES

Table 2.1	Definitions of circular economy	20
Table 2.2	Barriers to the circular economy	26
Table 3.1	Definitions of crowdfunding	39
Table 3.2	Examples of circularity projects financed through donation-based crowdfunding on various platforms	50
Table 3.3	Examples of circularity projects financed through reward-based crowdfunding across various platforms	52
Table 3.4	Examples of circularity projects financed through loan-based crowdfunding across various platforms	53
Table 3.5	Examples of circularity projects financed through equity crowdfunding across various platforms	55
Table 4.1	Non-exhaustive table of approaches to design for circularity	64
Table 4.2	Non-exhaustive table of approaches to design for circularity of the production and logistics process	70
Table 4.3	Descriptive statistics of identified projects	74
Table 5.1	Research comparing the likelihood of success for projects with sustainability or circularity features with projects with generalist features	88
Table 5.2	Research on the likelihood of success for projects with sustainability or circularity features	92
Table 5.3	Variables pertaining to the crowdfunding campaign	105
Table 5.4	Variables associated with financiers	106
Table 5.5	Variables related to communication	107

xiii

Table 5.6	Variables pertaining to the sustainability and/ or circularity dimensions of the project	108
Table 5.7	Variables related to the proponent, the proposing team, and their description	109
Table 5.8	Variables related to the description and presentation of the project	111
Table 5.9	Variables related to the reference market	111
Table 5.10	Variables related to the perceived quality and progress of the project	112
Table 6.1	Definitions of greenwashing	127
Table 6.2	Forms of product greenwashing implementation	130
Table 6.3	Forms of corporate greenwashing implementation	132
Table 7.1	Number of companies responding to the questionnaire that were established immediately after a crowdfunding campaign (inception stage), in the growth phase, and in the maturity phase	147
Table 7.2	Adoption of circularity strategies in companies established immediately after a crowdfunding campaign (startup phase), in companies utilizing crowdfunding during the growth phase, and in those in the maturity phase	153
Table 7.3	Adoption and interest in environmental certifications among companies formed immediately after a crowdfunding campaign (inception phase, growth phase, and maturity phase)	161

CHAPTER 1

Introduction

Abstract The transition toward sustainable socio-economic-technological systems is essential to address pressing environmental challenges. Issues such as biodiversity loss, waste generation, and resource depletion indeed threaten the planet's regenerative capacity. In response, the concepts of sustainability and, more recently, the circular economy have gained significant importance. Businesses play a crucial role in this transition. Enabling factors such as product design capabilities, creating collaborations and partnerships, and accessing and utilizing technologies can influence the magnitude and speed of implementing sustainability and circular economy strategies in companies. Among the enabling factors, access to financing plays a prominent role. This introductory chapter contextualizes crowdfunding within sustainability and circular economy issues and outlines the volume's structure.

Keywords Circular economy · Environmental sustainability · Crowdfunding · Businesses · Enablers

Today, the transition toward more sustainable socio-economic-technological systems represents an ever-increasing need for human society (Meadows et al., 2004). From an environmental perspective, the

© The Author(s), under exclusive license to Springer Nature
Switzerland AG 2024
F. Corsini and M. Frey, *Crowdfunding for Environmental Sustainability and the Circular Economy*,
https://doi.org/10.1007/978-3-031-66211-9_1

1

loss of biodiversity, pollution of air, water, and soil, and resource depletion are increasingly endangering the regenerative capacity of the planet. From a social viewpoint, problems such as unemployment, poor working conditions, intra and intergenerational equity, and the widening of inequalities are becoming more pronounced. At the same time, economic challenges for individual companies and entire economic systems are becoming increasingly acute, among these, for instance, are risks associated with sourcing and financial and economic instability (Sachs, 2015). To tackle these issues, the concept of sustainability, and subsequently that of circular economy, has gained ever-increasing importance on the agendas of policymakers, businesses, and citizens (Brennan et al., 2015).

In this context, the role of enterprises is essential for holistic sustainable development and the transition to a circular economy. The consideration of environmental issues in businesses, which can undoubtedly generate benefit and competitive advantage, depends on numerous factors. Some of these can be defined as enabling factors, that is, able to influence the magnitude and speed of implementing environmental strategies in the company's operations. Among the enabling factors are a company's ability to procure financing, its capability to design products with lesser environmental impacts, the ability to foresee market trends, and the evolution of consumer interests. In this context, this volume discusses the instrument of crowdfunding as an enabling factor for the corporate transition toward environmental sustainability and the circular economy. Specifically, as described in the volume, crowdfunding can provide businesses with the necessary economic resources and overcome liquidity-related issues; at the same time, crowdfunding not only helps finance projects but also offers a means to pre-sell unfinished products and contribute to marketing and corporate image. Furthermore, it allows for a better understanding of consumer preferences and facilitates co-creation through feedback from funders to incorporate solutions capable of reducing the environmental impacts of products. This introductory chapter contextualizes crowdfunding within issues related to environmental sustainability and the circular economy and also aims to present the structure of the volume.

1.1   Sustainability and the Circular Economy

The root of the term "sustainability" can be traced back to the French verb "soutenir," meaning "to uphold," predominantly used in the forestry sector. This referred to the principle that the quantity of timber harvested should not surpass its capacity for regrowth (Brown et al., 1987). Later, this term found its place in the realm of ecology, symbolizing the principle that calls for respecting nature's regenerative abilities. More contemporarily, the concept is associated with the mounting evidence of global environmental risks. Such risks have been systematically scrutinized since the 1960s, eliciting questions about trends in production and consumption, and their future maintainability (Jackson, 2009). The 1972 Stockholm Conference and the report "The Limits to Growth" had significant repercussions, particularly in interpreting development and environment as elements in stark contradiction to each other (Sachs, 2015). The Brundtland Report (1987) revisited this opposition, stating that "the concept of sustainable development implies limits—not absolute limits, but limitations imposed by the current state of technology and social organization on environmental resources and the biosphere's capacity to absorb the effects of human activities" (Brundtland, 1987, p.8). In the same context, the Brundtland Commission also provided the most commonly accepted definition of sustainability as "development that meets the needs of the present without compromising the ability of future generations to meet their own needs" (Brundtland, 1987). While the term sustainable development was initially intended as a response to environmental issues and concerns, it has since embraced a broader spectrum of meanings. In particular, this perspective was superseded in 1992 at the First United Nations Conference on Environment and Development (UNCED, 1992) in Rio de Janeiro, from which the Rio Declaration on Environment and Development and the local implementation instrument known as Agenda 21 emerged, affirming the multidimensional nature of sustainability. This articulated the meaning of environmental sustainability as ecosystem protection, economic sustainability as productive use of resources, and social sustainability as defending human rights, fighting poverty, distributive equity, and safeguarding health.

Today, the most widely recognized interpretation of sustainable development presupposes the so-called "triple bottom line" identifying three pillars of sustainability: economic, social, and environmental (Elkington, 1997). These three dimensions of sustainability are tightly interwoven and interconnected, continuously influencing each other and acting as interdependent pillars capable of mutually reinforcing each other (UN, 2005).

In addressing facets of environmental sustainability, the notion of a circular economy, although not entirely fresh as illustrated in Chapter 2, has recently taken a prominent place in policymakers' agendas, beginning with the first European circular economy package (European Commission, 2015). The Ellen MacArthur Foundation gave the most renowned definition of a circular economy, describing it as "an industrial economy that is restorative or regenerative by intention and design" (2013, p. 14). In consonance with the concept of sustainable development, the circular economy also underscores the finite nature of planetary resources, spotlighting problems of a global scale which consequently lead to collective responsibilities and the importance of cooperation among various players (Geissdoerfer et al., 2017). Both concepts often engage interdisciplinary approaches to incorporate non-economic aspects more effectively into the vision of development and guide the actions of different stakeholders. They both depend significantly on regulation and the creation of tools that incentivize the transition of economic players (Geissdoerfer et al., 2017). In fact, both sustainability and the circular economy highlight the private sector's role in the transition, considering it possesses greater capabilities and resources than any other player. Specifically, a growing body of research underscores the importance of business model innovation as key to the necessary socio-economic-technological transitions (Geissdoerfer et al., 2016).

The objectives encompassed by the two paradigms are incredibly similar, but the objectives underlying the concept of sustainability are broader in scope than those of the circular economy. Sustainability aims to create benefits for the environment (i.e., pollution reduction, combating climate change, waste reduction, etc.), the economy, and society (i.e., defending human rights, fighting poverty, distributive equity, protecting human health) as a whole (Elkington, 1997). In contrast, the main underlying benefits of the circular economy are of an economic nature for the system's actors (i.e., cost reduction and revenue generation from circular activities), but also environmental (i.e., mainly related to resource savings and waste reduction) and social (e.g., job creation).

Therefore, although the notions of sustainability and the circular economy bear significant similarities, numerous scholars perceive the circular economy as either a prerequisite or an instrument to realize sustainable development (Geissdoerfer et al., 2017; Walker et al., 2022).

1.2 The Role of Corporations and Enabling Factors for the Transition

Businesses are instrumental in sustainable growth and circular transition. Hence, corporate management becomes a crucial determinant in molding the future of firms, the economy, and society at large. Such managerial actions are based on decisions steered by measures like visions and strategies, which have the power to sketch the company's business model and its organizational progression. Strategies that can incorporate environmental considerations are fundamentally important for sustainable development and the circular transition, and also for successfully steering a company through a continuously evolving ecosystem of social, legal, political, and economic requirements. However, companies today are still not entirely focused on placing sustainability at the heart of their business strategy, erroneously believing the costs outweigh the benefits.

In numerous instances, conventional business models focus on generating value primarily for shareholders, often to the detriment of other involved parties. The concept of "shared value creation" was brought to light by Porter and Kramer (2002), suggesting that companies can cultivate economic value by pinpointing and addressing social issues that intersect with their business operations. Enterprises that succeed in reshaping the corporate ecosystem through designing models that yield value for all stakeholders, encompassing employees, shareholders, supply chains, civil society, and the environment, unquestionably gain advantages. The strategic value of sustainability significantly derives from stakeholder engagement, enabling companies to foresee and respond to economic, social, environmental, and regulatory changes more swiftly. The challenge in forging relationships with crucial stakeholders could escalate conflicts and amplify operational difficulties.

Global supply chain vulnerability is another crucial aspect in corporate strategies (Sarkis et al., 2011). Factors like climate change, resource scarcity, and subpar working conditions in several regions worldwide escalate the supply risks for businesses. As a result, strategic decisions necessitate the formulation of long-term adaptive capacities, encompassing sustainability aspects within corporate functions. Inclusion of sustainability within corporate strategies goes beyond merely serving as a risk management instrument; it also acts as a catalyst for innovation. Recrafting products to comply with environmental standards or societal needs presents fresh business prospects (Schaltegger & Wagner, 2011).

Currently, a transformation in consumer consciousness is evident, with a heightened demand for increased transparency from companies, coupled with a burgeoning interest in environmental issues.

Contemporary consumers increasingly attribute value to companies that are attentive to environmental aspects (Kostadinova, 2016). Some studies underscore post-recession consumers' shift in buying decisions toward products offered by companies devoted to social and environmental issues (Fink & Whelan, 2016).

Beyond these advantages, considering issues related to sustainability can also enhance the attraction and retention of corporate personnel (Benn et al., 2015). Companies investing in sustainability initiatives tend to foster a stronger culture and engagement than those where these aspects are not considered. Companies that incorporate sustainability into their business strategy recognize employees as principal stakeholders who are proud to work for companies cognizant of pursuing broader objectives.

Although the benefits of incorporating sustainability considerations into businesses are clear, the adoption of such strategies also depends on a series of enabling factors. Enabling factors represent the tools that can influence the magnitude and speed of implementing sustainability and circular economy strategies in companies (Danese et al., 2019). In some contexts, enabling factors can also influence the continuation of a certain type of business strategy. The main enabling factors include the top management's commitment and the ability to utilize certain technologies.

The implementation of business models and strategies considering environmental issues is certainly enabled by the interest and commitment of corporate leaders. Top management defines the organization's strategic vision, identifies priorities, and allocates resources. Furthermore, top management can create and maintain a corporate culture that encourages sustainability and the necessary innovation to incorporate environmental issues into daily business operations (Wong et al., 2016). Fundamental is the ability to effectively communicate the company's vision and commitment toward such themes by the top management, to engage all levels of the organization, create a corporate culture that supports decisions and strategies and engenders trust among all stakeholders. The top management's commitment toward these topics is also evidenced by "leading by example" approaches, namely their ability to demonstrate practical personal commitment to sustainability and circular economy, which can have a significant impact on the behavior of other corporate managers and all employees.

Creating collaborations and partnerships is essential to accelerate the adoption of sustainability strategies and circular economy in businesses (Grzybowska, 2012). This approach is based on the fact that transitioning toward such models requires a systemic change that goes beyond individual organizations and necessitates collaboration among multiple actors. Partnerships can take various forms. Collaboration can occur with other businesses, for example within the supply chain, to test new types of sustainable materials or co-design products following eco-design principles. The ability to create partnerships can also be directed toward collaboration with non-profit organizations, academic institutions, governmental bodies, or other stakeholders; such approaches can enable knowledge and skill sharing or the implementation of research and development projects. The ability to form partnerships can also aid businesses in accessing new markets, technologies, or funding sources, as well as managing risks associated with the supply chain, such as the volatility of raw material prices.

Another enabling factor is the ability to access and utilize technologies. In this context, digital technologies, like the Internet of Things (IoT), blockchain, Artificial Intelligence (AI), and data analytics, can be particularly relevant. Notably, several studies in the literature have described digitization as a driving force for transitioning toward adopting sustainability and circular economy strategies (Kintscher et al., 2020). For instance, technologies can enhance workers' skills and abilities and assist them in making operational decisions, such as promoting eco-design by providing data-based instructions. Real-time processed data can predict demand and help manage inventory, minimizing production waste and improving the sustainability of the manufacturing process. Companies capable of leveraging digital technologies can also improve logistics from a sustainability perspective and reduce supply chain-related risks.

Among many, the final enabling factor is the ability to secure financing (Alayón et al., 2022). In the current context, traditional financial tools are only minimally capable of supporting the transition in businesses as they are not fully aligned with the goals of sustainability and circular economy. In recent years, an increasingly wide range of green bonds, sustainable investment funds, etc., is becoming prevalent, but these are only available to a limited number of companies. Funding instruments such as those from the European Union can be used to support large-scale transition projects that require substantial investments. While the tools provided by the private and public sectors to finance the transition process are undoubtedly relevant, these can be further supplemented by other forms of financing in a landscape where diverse financing opportunities can contribute to the realization of varied projects related to environmental issues. Among these, crowdfunding can be seen as a valid alternative to existing financing opportunities on the market to realize projects connected to environmental sustainability and the circular economy by providing companies with the necessary financial resources. As discussed in the volume, crowdfunding can not only provide companies with the necessary economic resources, but it can also help them integrate strategies to improve product environmental performance (eco-design), environmental marketing, and even creating communities to support the adoption of alternative business models, such as product-as-a-service. In the near future, considering the growing use of this tool, it is expected to have an even more significant impact, for companies able to fully exploit its potential, in facilitating sustainability and circularity strategies and objectives.

1.3 VOLUME STRUCTURE

The Chapter 2 of the volume delves into the paradigm of the circular economy, highlighting the main barriers that companies encounter in the transition and identifying the factors that facilitate its adoption and implementation. By the end of this chapter, crowdfunding is identified as a tool capable of reducing barriers to circular transition in businesses.

The Chapter 3 introduces the topic of crowdfunding and its evolution from its origins to the present. The chapter also describes the functioning of crowdfunding platforms and the four types of crowdfunding (donation, reward, loan, and equity).

The Chapter 4 explores the topic of eco-design for circularity and analyzes the contribution of reward-based crowdfunding platforms as financial instruments to support the development of products designed to be circular.

The Chapter 5 analyzes one of the scientific research streams that has attracted much interest since the dawn of crowdfunding, concerning the success of crowdfunding campaigns. In particular, the chapter focuses on the analysis of research trying to identify the various success factors that can influence a crowdfunding campaign in relation to projects connected with the environment.

The Chapter 6 examines the issue of fraud in crowdfunding, with particular emphasis on the phenomenon of greenwashing. This occurs when projects present themselves as sustainable, even when they are not, thus deceiving investors interested in supporting initiatives of this type. Such fraudulent behavior can cause environmental damage and undermine the reputation of crowdfunding, compromising investor trust.

The Chapter 7 aims to explore the role of crowdfunding in the organizational life cycle of companies. Sometimes, a crowdfunding campaign may represent the beginning of an entrepreneurial journey, at other times it may be used in phases of business growth or maturity to test new products or finance new projects. Even from a sustainability perspective, a crowdfunding campaign can represent a company's first experimentation with a project, or be part of a process already underway for some time. In this context, the chapter delves into the circularity strategies implemented by companies that use crowdfunding in the various stages of the organizational cycle.

Ultimately, the book's final chapter offers a series of concluding observations.

References

Alayón, C. L., Säfsten, K., & Johansson, G. (2022). Barriers and enablers for the adoption of sustainable manufacturing by manufacturing SMEs. *Sustainability, 14*(4), 2364.

Benn, S., Teo, S. T., & Martin, A. (2015). Employee participation and engagement in working for the environment. *Personnel Review, 44*(4), 492–510.

Brennan, G., Tennant, M., & Blomsma, F. (2015). Business and production solutions: Closing the loop. In H. Kopnina & E. Shoreman-Ouimet (Eds.), *Sustainability: Key issues* (pp. 219–239). Routledge.

Brown, B. J., Hanson, M. E., Liverman, D. M., & Merideth, R. W., Jr. (1987). Global sustainability: Toward definition. *Environmental ManagEment, 11*(6), 713–719.

Brundtland, G. H., Khalid, M., Agnelli, S., Al-Athel, S. A., Chidzero, B. J. N. Y., Fadika, L. M., & Singh, N. (1987). *Our common future.* World Commission on Environment and Development.

Danese, P., Lion, A., & Vinelli, A. (2019). Drivers and enablers of supplier sustainability practices: A survey-based analysis. *International Journal of Production Research, 57*(7), 2034–2056.

Elkington, J. (1997). *Cannibals with forks: The triple bottom line of 21st century.* Capstone.

Ellen MacArthur Foundation. (2013). *Towards the circular economy* (Vol. 2). Isle of Wight.

European Commission. (2015). *Closing the Loop - An EU Action Plan for the Circular Economy*, Brussels. Available at: https://eur-lex.europa.eu/resource.html?uri=cellar:8a8ef5e8-99a0-11e5-b3b7-01aa75ed71a1.0012.02/DOC_1&format=PDF. Accessed on 22 June 2023.

Fink, C., & Whelan, T. (2016). *The sustainability business case for the 21st century corporation.*

Geissdoerfer, M., Bocken, N. M., & Hultink, E. J. (2016). Design thinking to enhance the sustainable business modelling process—A workshop based on a value mapping process. *Journal of Cleaner Production, 135*, 1218–1232.

Geissdoerfer, M., Savaget, P., Bocken, N. M., & Hultink, E. J. (2017). The Circular Economy—A new sustainability paradigm? *Journal of Cleaner Production, 143*, 757–768.

Grzybowska, K. (2012). Sustainability in the supply chain: Analysing the enablers. *Environmental Issues in Supply Chain Management: New Trends and Applications*, 25–40.

Jackson, T. (2009). *Prosperity without growth. Economics for a finite planet.* Earthscan.

Kintscher, L., Lawrenz, S., Poschmann, H., & Sharma, P. (2020). Recycling 4.0—digitalization as a key for the advanced circular economy. *J. Communication, 15*(9), 652–660.

Kostadinova, E. (2016). Sustainable consumer behavior: Literature overview. *Economic Alternatives, 2*, 224–234.

Meadows, D. H., Randers, J., & Meadows, D. L. (2004). *The limits to growth. The 30-year update.* Routledge.

Porter, M. E., & Kramer, M. R. (2002). The competitive advantage of corporate philanthropy. *Harvard Business Review, 80*(12), 56–68.

Sachs, J. (2015). *The age of sustainable development.* Columbia University Press.

Sarkis, J., Zhu, Q., & Lai, K. H. (2011). An organizational theoretic review of green supply chain management literature. *International Journal of Production Economics, 130*(1), 1–15.

Schaltegger, S., & Wagner, M. (2011). Sustainable entrepreneurship and sustainability innovation: Categories and interactions. *Business Strategy and the Environment, 20*(4), 222–237.

UNCED. (1992). *United Nations conference on environment and development, the Rio de Janeiro declaration.*

UN. (2005). Resolution adopted by the general assembly 60/1. 2005 world summit outcome. *Sixtieth Session. Agenda Items, 46.*

Walker, A. M., Opferkuch, K., Roos Lindgreen, E., Raggi, A., Simboli, A., Vermeulen, W. J., & Salomone, R. (2022). What is the relation between circular economy and sustainability? Answers from front-runner companies engaged with circular economy practices. *Circular Economy and Sustainability, 2*(2), 731–758.

Wong, J. K. W., San Chan, J. K., & Wadu, M. J. (2016). Facilitating effective green procurement in construction projects: An empirical study of the enablers. *Journal of Cleaner Production, 135*, 859–871.

CHAPTER 2

The Paradigm of the Circular Economy: Barriers and Enabling Factors for Companies

Abstract The paradigm of circular economy underscores that the "take-make-dispose" model of production and consumption is no longer sustainable. The chapter introduces the concept of circular economy, presenting its theoretical and conceptual foundations, along with the various European policies that have prioritized this transition. The shift toward a circular economy model, which considers businesses as one of the key players, is not immune to barriers. These barriers include technological constraints, regulatory complexities, and cultural resistance, all of which hinder the adoption of circular strategies in businesses. Among the main barriers, one of the most significant is the financial challenge, exemplified by the high initial investment costs necessary to support the transition in businesses. In this context, crowdfunding is presented as an enabling tool for the circular transition in companies.

Keywords Circular economy paradigm · Enablers · Barriers · Financial barrier · Crowdfunding

© The Author(s), under exclusive license to Springer Nature Switzerland AG 2024
F. Corsini and M. Frey, *Crowdfunding for Environmental Sustainability and the Circular Economy*,
https://doi.org/10.1007/978-3-031-66211-9_2

2.1 The Need for a New Production and Consumption Paradigm

Since the first industrial revolution, global economic growth has proceeded in lockstep with the utilization of materials. This growth model took place, especially after the Second World War, a historical period marked by a global demographic boom and the advent of consumer society, that has profoundly reshaped the United States and European countries, modifying people's lifestyle to become more sophisticated, demanding, and modern (Cavazza, 2018). The current development model can be referred to as a "take-make-dispose" model, a term that implies the notion of raw materials being extracted from the biosphere, transformed into products, and then turned into waste. The unsustainable nature of this strategy is clear upon data analysis. In 1972, the Club of Rome's report, "The Limits of Growth," cautioned about unsustainable resource handling and the potential for a sudden, uncontrolled decrease in population and industrial potential, with the consumption of natural resources at 28.6 billion tons (Fraser et al., 2023). The "Circularity Gap Report" showed in 2021 that global economies used over 100 billion tons (101 Gt) of natural resources. The trend related to global resource extraction is presented in Fig. 2.1.

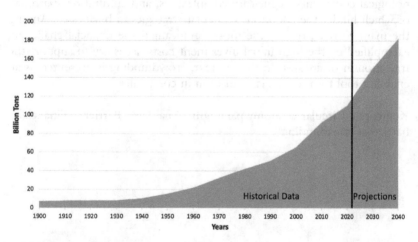

Fig. 2.1 Extraction of raw materials from the biosphere (*Source* Adapted from The World Bank, 2022)

Waste creation is inextricably tied to the expansion of raw material exploitation from the biosphere. According to the "Circularity Gap Report" data, 32.6 billion tons of waste were produced worldwide in 2021; more than a third of this goes directly to landfill. Only 8.6 billion tons were reintroduced into the global production system through energy recovery and recycling processes (Fraser et al., 2023). Waste, and its frequently inadequate management in certain regions of the globe, constitute one of the primary sources of health, environmental, social, and economic burdens.

The link between the usage of materials, the generation of waste, and climate change is unmistakable. As per the data from the United Nations' "Emission Gap Report," approximately 70% of all global emissions are associated with the use, handling, and end-of-life treatment of resources (UNEP, 2022). The excessive removal of resources from the biosphere and subsequent waste production is diminishing the natural capital. The repercussions of our goods and services creation processes on ecosystems and their vital functions, such as biodiversity and resilience to extreme weather, are obvious. Rapid material extraction and waste production have been pinpointed as key factors behind our ongoing environmental strain. The cycle of material management—encompassing extraction, manufacturing, transportation, consumption, and disposal—is currently responsible for 90% of total biodiversity loss (Ellen MacArthur Foundation, 2023).

The current linear model of "take-make-dispose" indicates that by 2060, we will require at least two Earths to satisfy material demands and manage the global waste output. Unless we can significantly separate economic expansion from resource consumption, environmental stress, economic risks, and inequalities will only escalate (The World Bank, 2022).

2.2　The Paradigm of Circular Economy

The circular economy idea has gained traction over the past ten years as a strategy for increasing prosperity worldwide, limiting resource extraction and consumption, and consequently reducing waste production. The circular economy model, embodied in a variety of policies and business strategies, strives to augment resource efficiency by changing production-consumption systems into self-perpetuating cycles, thus reducing extraction, waste, and corresponding environmental impacts. This concept draws from multiple theoretical underpinnings.

Among them, the circular economy derives from the notion of "industrial ecology," which, along with the related concept of "industrial symbiosis," was first used in economic geography in the 1940s to clarify the crucial factors influencing the location of industries for the most efficient use of resources and waste minimization. The aim of industrial ecology is to foster cyclic processes where the waste of one firm morphs into raw materials for others, adhering to the principle of industrial symbiosis. It utilizes a systemic approach to design productive systems that cohabit with local natural ecosystems, while being aware of their global repercussions. Within this field of eco-economic literature, Boulding's (1966) work serves as a crucial reference. His work has a significant influence on the ideas and tenets that guide contemporary circular economy thinking. Regarding materials, energy, and information/knowledge in particular, Boulding (1966) considers the distinction between open and closed systems. These components serve as the foundation for the economic system that the author describes as "a material process that involves the discovery and extraction of fossil fuels and raw materials, and at the other end, a process through which these resources are dumped into non-economic reservoirs." Essentially, this represents a depiction of the economic system that closely resembles what is now referred to as the linear or "take-make-dispose" economy. The author also postulates the significance of rethinking the economic growth model, which, in his opinion, should primarily center around the "maintenance of stocks." This stands in contrast to economists of his era who held the belief that production, consumption, and hence the generation of gross domestic product, offer a suitable and sufficient gauge for sustainable growth.

The circular economy also draws from the work of Stahel (1982), who underscores "prolonging the life of goods" as the initial step toward a gradual shift to a sustainable society that aligns progress with the planet's limited resource pool. Stahel is the pioneer in visually defining the circular economy as depicted in many current illustrations. Stahel's proposed economic model is exemplified by a spiral system that curbs material usage, energy flow, and environmental deterioration without impeding economic expansion or social and technical advancement (Fig. 2.2). To

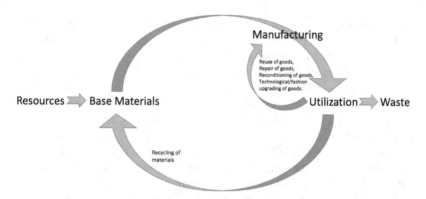

Fig. 2.2 First schematic representation of a circular economic system (*Source* Adapted from Stahel, 1982)

achieve this result, it is necessary to carry out some activities including reuse, repair, refurbishment, product upgrades, and material recycling.

Pearce and Turner (1990) originally outlined the concept of the circular economy, distinguishing between natural systems (circular) and economic systems (linear). They emphasized the importance of viewing Earth as a closed economic system in which economy and ecology are interconnected through circular linkages, adhering to the idea that "everything is an input for everything else," influenced by Boulding's (1966) principles. Based on this presumption, they analyzed the conventional linear economic system and proposed the circular economy as an alternative, invoking the first and second laws of thermodynamics.[1]

A burgeoning body of literature from various fields has shaped our understanding and perception of the circular economy in recent years (Lieder & Rashid, 2016). Notably, literature related to industrial ecology has been particularly influential, advocating for a systematic strategy that takes a comprehensive view of human economic activity and environmental sustainability (Garner & Keoleian, 1995). This literature

---

[1] Since no matter nor energy can be generated or destroyed, according to the first law of thermodynamics, any natural resource that has been used will eventually return to the environment as solid waste or emissions. The second law of thermodynamics states that there are intrinsic physical limitations that prevent the construction of a system in which all waste may be perfectly efficiently recycled and transformed into natural resources (Pearce & Turner, 1990).

underscores the importance of innovative product design and manufacturing in reintegrating materials once deemed as waste back into the production cycle. Industrial symbiosis, a practical application of industrial ecology principles at the organizational level, encourages mutually beneficial partnerships for the exchange of resources and by-products (Chertow, 2000). These collaborations can extend beyond geographical proximity and foster networks for knowledge sharing and the cultivation of eco-innovation.

The "cradle-to-cradle" design concept has also significantly influenced the current understanding of the circular economy (Braungart et al., 2007). This approach aims to preserve and enhance the value, quality, and usefulness of material resources to create a net positive environmental impact, in contrast to traditional sustainability strategies focused on reducing negative environmental consequences. This strategy distinguishes between biological and technical materials—each can be optimized through product design, production methods, and supply chains. Technical materials, being durable, can cycle endlessly within a closed-loop system, while biological materials, being biodegradable, can be safely returned to the environment after use. For retaining or increasing the value and efficiency of these resources, actors within the value chain must leverage knowledge gained through flow networks (Braungart et al., 2007).

Furthermore, the concept of product-service systems, first introduced in the mid-1990s (Tukker, 2015), has profoundly affected our present conception of the circular economy. Product-service systems, as defined by Tukker and Tischner (2006), blend tangible goods with intangible services designed and integrated to meet the needs of the end-user. These systems prioritize the functionality or overall satisfaction desired by customers as a basis for business growth.

Drawing from these sources, the Ellen MacArthur Foundation formulated an early definition of the contemporary circular economy, releasing three studies in 2013, including the now-iconic "butterfly" diagram. According to the Ellen MacArthur Foundation (2013), the circular economy is described as an industrial economy that is deliberately restorative and aims to imitate nature by actively refining and optimizing the systems in which it operates. It is an economy designed to be restorative and regenerative, continuously maximizing the utility and value of products, components, and materials through technical and biological cycles. Indeed, material flows within industrial processes are categorized into two cycles: the biological cycle, where materials are designed to safely reintegrate into the biosphere, and the technical cycle, where materials circulate while preserving their quality and without negatively impacting the biosphere. The higher the purity and quality of these material flows, the greater the added value generated by the circular economy. The fundamental objective is to enable effective flows of materials, energy, labor, and information to restore natural and social capital (Ellen MacArthur Foundation, 2013).

While the definition provided by the Ellen MacArthur Foundation (2013) is widely used to depict the circular economy, there is no universally agreed-upon definition in the literature. For instance, Kirchherr et al. (2017) discovered 114 definitions of the circular economy in their research. A selection of these definitions is presented in Table 2.1.

Present definitions of the circular economy underscore several aligned objectives. Firstly, the circular economy acknowledges that products or assets should not be wasted or discarded prematurely, aiming to preserve their value for as long as possible. Secondly, it strives to progressively eradicate waste by intervening at various stages of a product's life cycle, including during the design and manufacturing processes to ensure materials and resources are utilized efficiently and effectively. Thirdly, the circular economy advocates for resource conservation by eliminating inefficiencies throughout the entire production and consumption cycle. In essence, it seeks to foster a system that is both sustainable and efficient by maximizing resource use and minimizing waste. Lastly, the circular economy aims to stimulate innovation by embracing new business models and paradigms that reduce the harmful impacts of production and consumption on the environment. That is, it endeavors to make industries and processes more environmentally friendly and sustainable through the encouragement of innovative approaches (Kirchherr et al., 2017).

The diversity of meanings attributed to the circular economy has cast doubt on the viability of the concept itself. Critics, such as those presented in the paper by Corvellec et al. (2022), argue that the circular economy may be ideologically driven and faces practical and theoretical challenges in truly achieving sustainability goals. These discussions serve as a critical backdrop in exploring the concept of the circular economy, reminding us of the complexities and nuances involved in implementing circular strategies effectively. In particular, it highlights the necessity to recognize and address the inherent challenges of transitioning to a circular economy.

Table 2.1 Definitions of circular economy

Definition	Source
"A circular economy is an industrial system that is restorative or regenerative by intention and design. It replaces the end-of-life concept with restoration, shifts towards the use of renewable energy, eliminates the use of toxic chemicals, which impair reuse and return to the biosphere, and aims for the elimination of waste through the superior design of materials, products, systems and business models. Such an economy is based on a few simple principles. First, at its core, a circular economy aims to design out waste. Waste does not exist: products are designed and optimized for a cycle of disassembly and reuse. These tight component and product cycles define the circular economy and set it apart from disposal and even recycling, where large amounts of embedded energy and labour are lost. Second, circularity introduces a strict differentiation between consumable and durable components of a product."	Ellen MacArthur Foundation (2013, p. 15)
"A circular economy is a system which maintains the value of products, materials and resources in the economy for as long as possible, and minimises the generation of waste. This means a system where products are reused, repaired, remanufactured or recycled."	European Commission (2015)
"Circular economy mainly emerges in the literature through three main actions, i.e. the so called 3R's Principles: Reduction, Reuse and Recycle"	Ghisellini et al. (2016, p. 4)
The circular economy is "an industrial system that is restorative or regenerative by intention and design. It replaces the 'end-of-life' concept with restoration, shifts towards the use of renewable energy, eliminates the use of toxic chemicals, which impair reuse, and aims for the elimination of waste through the superior design of materials, products, systems, and, within this, business models."	Geissdoerfer et al. (2017, p. 759)
"The concept of circular economy conceives of a production and consumption system with minimal losses of materials and energy through extensive reuse, recycling, and recovery."	Haupt et al. (2017, p. 615)

(continued)

Table 2.1 (continued)

Definition	Source
The circular economy is "an economic system that replaces the 'end-of-life' concept with reducing, alternatively reusing, recycling and recovering materials in production/distribution and consumption processes. It operates at the micro level (products, companies, consumers), meso level (eco-industrial parks) and macro level (city, region, nation and beyond), with the aim to accomplish sustainable development, thus simultaneously creating environmental quality, economic prosperity and social equity, to the benefit of current and future generations. It is enabled by novel business models and responsible consumers. We hope that this CE definition can be a contribution to the scholarly CE community with this definition ideally serving as a conceptual foundation for future work on the topic."	Kirchherr et al. (2017, p. 228)
"Circular economy is an economy constructed from societal production-consumption systems that maximise the service produced from the linear nature-society-nature material and energy throughput flow."	Korhonen et al. (2018, p. 547)
The circular economy is a regenerative production-consumption system that aims to maintain extraction rates of resources and generation rates of wastes and emissions under suitable values for planetary boundaries, by closing the system, reducing its size, and maintaining the resource's value as long as possible within the system, mainly leaning on design and education, and with capacity to be implemented at any scale	Suarez-Eiroa et al. (2019, p. 960)
"Circular Economy (CE) is an activity, set of process for reducing the material used in production and consumption, promoting material resilience, closing loops and exchange sustainability offering in such a way that maximize the ecological system."	Awan et al. (2020, p. 17)

Source Authors' elaboration

2.3 Circular Economy in European Policies

With its deep roots in the sustainability, the European Union's political discourse has long included a discussion of the shift to the circular economy. The term "circular economy" has emerged in European policies since 2015, the year the seminal circular economy package was unveiled. This package, suggesting a modification to certain European directives, primarily endeavored to transform waste management toward enhancing recycling. The legislation prioritizes the waste hierarchy approach, with prevention and reuse as foremost measures, followed by material recovery such as composting and energy recovery, and landfill disposal only as the final resort.

The package aimed to amend the Waste Framework Directive in order to establish challenging goals for recycling and preparing municipal waste for reuse, and it urged member states to implement distinct collecting methods for organic and textile waste. The 2015 circular economy package also aimed to update the packaging directives by setting new recycling targets for packaging waste, while the revision of the WEEE directive set new targets for the segregated collection and recycling of e-waste. Finally, the amendment to the landfill directive, also part of the same package, put forth an aim to curb the fraction of urban waste relegated to landfill.[2]

The European Commission's adoption of a plastics strategy also represented a crucial step in the transition to a circular economy. This initiative aims to rethink the design, manufacture, usage, and recycling of plastic goods within the member states. Launched at the beginning of 2018, the strategy is committed to rendering recycling a lucrative business venture, curtailing the generation of plastic waste, and fostering innovation and investment in this arena.

Later, the European Green Deal of 2019 made the transition toward a circular economy a top priority. In this charter, EU policy ties the concepts of sustainability and circularity into their long-term economic plans. The Circular Economy Action Plan of 2020 offers a product-centric policy framework with the goals of enhancing product design, bolstering

---

[2] The key elements of the amended directives aim to achieve: a common EU-level target of recycling 65% of municipal waste by 2030; a common EU-level target of recycling 75% of packaging waste by 2030; and a binding target to limit landfilling to a maximum of 10% of all waste by 2030.

the positions of consumers and public purchasers, and encouraging circularity in production. This plan places special emphasis on seven major product value chains that are known for using a lot of resources and having the potential to be circular: electronics and ICT, batteries and vehicles, packaging, plastics and textiles, buildings and construction, food, water, and nutrients.

At present, the most recent policy suggestions regarding the circular economy are turning the focus upstream to products designed for circularity right from the inception. Specifically, with the introduction of a new regulation on environmentally friendly product design in March 2022, the European Commission has laid out a framework that allows it to set circularity requirements for nearly all categories of goods entering the Union's market. This regulatory schema includes performance and information requirements like product lifespan, reusability, upgradability, repairability, and recyclability, among others. This method will facilitate the adoption of specific measures for products based on dedicated impact assessments.

The Commission has also launched particular initiatives to help the action plan's prioritized value chains make the transition to a circular economy. For instance, a novel approach was recently implemented to make textile goods more circular, making them stronger, more repairable, more reusable, and more recyclable. This plan aims to address the problems with fast fashion and the destruction of unsold textiles while making sure that their production completely complies with social rights.[3]

Further specific initiatives have been launched to support the transition within the construction sector. Notably, the proposed revision of the construction products legislation aims to strengthen the internal market for such products and to ensure that the regulatory framework drives the industry toward achieving the environmental sustainability goals set by the Green Deal.

Additional recent initiatives by the Commission aim to establish rules to empower consumers in the ecological transition, so they are better informed about the environmental sustainability of products and against misleading practices such as greenwashing.[4]

---

[3] EU strategy for sustainable and circular textiles Disponibile available at the following link: https://environment.ec.europa.eu/strategy/textiles-strategy_en.

[4] Environmental performance of products and businesses—demonstrating the truthfulness of claims. Available at the link: https://ec.europa.eu/info/law/better-regulation/have-your-say/initiatives/12511-Environmental-performance-of-products-and-businesses-demonstrating-the-truthfulness-of-claims_en.

Lastly, it is noteworthy to mention the various endeavors undertaken by the Commission to facilitate the influx of capital for companies interested in investing in strategies and business models pertaining to the circular economy. Among these initiatives, the Taxonomy Regulation, adopted in 2020, represents a pivotal action. This regulation institutes a classification scheme for economic endeavors, purposed to assess the environmental sustainability of investments and guide them toward projects and technologies that foster the goals of the Green Deal. An economic activity or project may be recognized as environmentally sustainable if it fosters at least one of the following objectives: alleviating climate change, adapting to climate changes, guaranteeing the sustainable usage and protection of water and marine resources, pivoting to a circular economy with an emphasis on waste prevention and heightened usage of secondary raw materials, curtailing and mitigating pollution, and preserving and regenerating biodiversity and ecosystems.

2.4 Barriers to Circularity

While corporations are beginning to explore strategies for introducing circular solutions and business models, the shift toward this circular paradigm is still nascent. Indeed, they encounter numerous obstacles in speeding up the propagation of circular strategies and business models. In some instances, technological constraints are often blamed for the limited progress in adoption. Some academics emphasize problems like a lack of technologies that are appropriate for the circular economy or a lack of technical know-how needed to carry out circular economy practices when discussing these kinds of obstacles (Milios et al., 2018). Other scholars point to more specific technological barriers, like the challenge in standardizing production with materials sourced from recycling processes (Kinnunen & Kaksonen, 2019).

Economic and market barriers also impede the adoption of circular strategies in companies. Many authors emphasize, for instance, the high initial investment costs to adopt circular economy practices and long investment depreciation periods (Kirchherr et al., 2018). Concurrently, the lack of public incentives for virtuous companies further discourages the adoption of such practices.

Another impactful type of barriers companies face are institutional and regulatory ones. Again, these barriers vary: some authors highlight, for example, the presence of uninspiring innovation policies (Masi et al.,

2018) that also slow the adoption of innovative environmental initiatives by companies; others underline the complexity of regulations (Tura et al., 2019) and even legislation that greatly complicates the implementation of circular strategies (de Jesus & Mendonça, 2018).

Social and cultural constraints also hinder the adoption of circular business models and strategies. In this case, examples of such barriers could relate to more general aspects such as the low priority of sustainability aspects in consumers' decision-making process (Rizos et al., 2015) or more specific aspects like the lack of appreciation for products made with circular materials such as secondary raw materials.[5]

The fifth and final family of barriers can be defined as corporate and supply chain barriers. Among these standout, for instance, the lack of involvement by corporate management (Mangla et al., 2018), the difficulty in creating a strong company culture on these issues (Kirchherr et al., 2018; Vanner et al., 2014), but also supply chain barriers, such as the absence of tools and collaboration networks on these issues (Tura et al., 2019).

Naturally, many of these barriers are strongly interconnected (Grafström & Aasma, 2021). The interrelation between the different barriers can lead to a chain reaction aimed at further inhibiting the transition process of companies. For instance, the inability to set an appropriate price for the use of virgin raw materials may inhibit the market for secondary raw materials, which may impede the development of effective waste separation and recycling technology. In this context, only through actions developed synergistically by various stakeholders, after having identified the main causes of the transition failure, can the trend be reversed.

Table 2.2 reconstructs the obstacles to the circular economy as they are discussed in the scholarly literature on the topic. These barriers have been collected through numerous studies conducted globally on the topic and are, therefore, not specific to a reference territorial context.

---

[5] The concept of secondary raw material was born to meet the legislator's need to find a balance between environmental protection and waste recovery in such a way as to enable its reintegration into the production cycle. In this context, the European legislation has stipulated that, under certain conditions, a substance classified as waste that undergoes a recovery operation may cease to be considered as such and will become a secondary raw material (SRM). Secondary raw materials, for instance, consist of materials derived from recycling processes that can be reintroduced into the economic system as new raw materials.

26   F. CORSINI AND M. FREY

Table 2.2   Barriers to the circular economy

Type of barriers	Details	Source
Technological Barriers	Shortage of diffusion of technologies for the circular economy	(Milios et al., 2018)
	Low quality of products made from recycled materials	(Milios et al., 2018)
	Absence of large-scale demonstrative projects	(Kirchherr et al., 2018)
	Lack of data on impacts	(Tura et al., 2019)
	Deficiency of know-how and technical skills for the implementation of circular economy practices	(Kirchherr et al., 2018; Vanner et al., 2014)
	Challenges in utilizing recycled materials on a large scale	(Kinnunen & Kaksonen, 2019)
	Ineffective technologies for material separation and recycling	(Kinnunen & Kaksonen, 2019)
	Difficult access to patents for the use of circular economy technologies	(Preston, 2012)
Economic and Market Barriers	High initial investment costs	(Kinnunen & Kaksonen, 2019; Kirchherr et al., 2018; Preston, 2012; Vanner et al., 2014)
	Absence of public incentives	(Tura et al., 2019; Vanner et al., 2014)
	Low raw material prices	(Kinnunen & Kaksonen, 2019; Kirchherr et al., 2018; Vanner et al., 2014)
	Difficulty in obtaining finance for investments in circular economy projects	(Kirchherr et al., 2018; Rizos et al., 2015)
	Long periods of investment amortization	(Kinnunen & Kaksonen, 2019)
	High logistical costs	(Kinnunen & Kaksonen, 2019)
	Low concentrations of valuable materials in recyclable materials	(Kinnunen & Kaksonen, 2019)
	Insignificant short-term returns	(Mangla et al., 2018)

(continued)

Table 2.2 (continued)

Type of barriers	Details	Source
	Uncertainty about the reliability of recycled material supply	(Masi et al., 2018)
	Economic benefits are poorly measurable	(Tura et al., 2019)
Institutional/Regulatory Barriers	Lock-in of linear infrastructures	(Kirchherr et al., 2018; Preston, 2012)
	Political obstacles to imposing an optimal price for resource use	(Preston, 2012)
	Weak institutional cooperation in circular economy initiatives and projects	(Preston, 2012)
	Limited incentives for public procurement	(Kirchherr et al., 2018; Vanner et al., 2014)
	Uninspiring innovation policies	(Masi et al., 2018)
	Poor policy coherence	(Vanner et al., 2014)
	Hindering laws and regulations	(de Jesus & Mendonça, 2018)
	Lack of support for financing, training, and fiscal policy	(Mangla et al., 2018)
	Overly strict regulations on some hazardous wastes that could be recycled	(Kinnunen & Kaksonen, 2019)
	Inconsistent regulations across various countries	(Kinnunen & Kaksonen, 2019)
	Absence of regulatory and fiscal pressure for the promotion of the circular economy	(Mangla et al., 2018)
	Recycling policies inadequate for high-quality use of recyclable materials	(Masi et al., 2018)
	Complex regulations	(Tura et al., 2019)
	Poor understanding by political decision-makers	(Tura et al., 2019)
	Lack of government support	(Rizos et al., 2015; Vanner et al., 2014)
Social and Cultural Barriers	Lack of awareness and interest among consumers	(Vanner et al., 2014)

(continued)

Table 2.2 (continued)

Type of barriers	Details	Source
	Underappreciation of products made from circular materials, especially those made from secondary raw materials	(Preston, 2012; Vanner et al., 2014)
	Low acceptance of sharing models by potential users	(Vanner et al., 2014)
	Lack of understanding of the benefits of the circular economy	(Rizos et al., 2015)
	Low priority in the consumer decision-making process	(Rizos et al., 2015)
	Inadequate comprehension of the concept of the circular economy	(Milios et al., 2018)
	Absence of a long-term vision among stakeholders	(Milios et al., 2018)
Internal Company Barriers and those related to the industry in which it operates	Difficulty in establishing measurable objectives in terms of the circular economy	(Kirchherr et al., 2018)
	Competition rather than cooperation within the supply chain and confidentiality	(Masi et al., 2018)
	Resistance from top management	(Agyemang et al., 2018)
	Risk aversion, weak management support, and acceptance of the business model	(Tura et al., 2019)
	Lack of involvement from middle management	(Mangla et al., 2018)
	Absent corporate culture on these topics	(Kirchherr et al., 2018; Vanner et al., 2014)
	Diverts attention from management	(Masi et al., 2018)
	Need for human resources specifically dedicated to circular economy activities	(Rizos et al., 2015)
	Poor cooperation between companies along the entire supply chain	(Agyemang et al., 2018; Kinnunen & Kaksonen, 2019; Kirchherr et al., 2018)

(continued)

Table 2.2 (continued)

Type of barriers	Details	Source
	Lack of training on these topics for human resource managers	(Rizos et al., 2015)
	Companies' inability to effectively manage reverse logistics	(Masi et al., 2018)
	Absence of supply chain collaboration networks	(Tura et al., 2019)
	Reluctance to cooperate along the supply chain	(Kirchherr et al., 2018)

Source Authors' elaboration

Considering the barriers mentioned previously, to effectively advance toward a circular economy, comprehensive strategies must be employed to overcome these barriers. These strategies may include harnessing technological innovations to improve recycling processes and material recovery, establishing economic incentives such as subsidies and tax benefits to lower the initial costs of circular economy projects and activities, and creating a supportive regulatory environment that simplifies and harmonizes rules to facilitate circular initiatives. Additionally, fostering a corporate culture that prioritizes sustainability and circular principles is crucial, as is actively engaging consumers through education and transparent marketing to increase their participation in circular systems. By integrating these strategies, policymakers, businesses, and consumers can build a resilient framework that supports the transition toward a circular economy.

2.5 How to Finance the Transition?

As evidenced from the preceding paragraph, the economic barriers are one of the main obstacles to adopting circular strategies and business models. Finding the right methods and resources to finance businesses' shift to the circular economy is thus essential.

The Next Generation EU Plan and funds from the EU's long-term budget are being used at the European level to rebuild the European economy after the epidemic and create a greener, fairer, and more technologically advanced Europe. The resources provided by these instruments amount to more than 2 trillion euros. At the same level, the issuance of bonds, including green bonds, and other additional financing measures were envisaged, such as a plastic tax on non-recycled packaging waste, to support the transition to the circular economy with those resources.

Not only are public resources necessary for the circular transition, but numerous private initiatives have also recently been launched to support circular strategies and business models in companies. Among these, numerous closed funds aim to invest in companies' circular economy projects.[6] For example, the Circular Innovation Fund is a private fund aimed at raising financial resources and directing them to support businesses that have invested in circular economy projects and are in a growth phase.[7]

Other instruments to support the financing of companies toward greater circularity include public equity funds. Among these are sectoral funds that allow investment in certain market sectors with the aim of pursuing revenue from trends expected to develop in the medium-long term. Among the many public equity funds that focus on investing in environmentally sustainable companies, the one launched by BlackRock in 2019, named the Circular Economy Public Equity Fund, is one of the most renowned.[8] The fund seeks to invest in publicly traded companies whose business structures and strategies reflect the concepts of the circular economy. The fund managed to surpass $2 billion in assets under management in 2021 after raising roughly $1 billion in its first year of operation.

Among the entities that provide financing in support of companies for the circular economy, the European Investment Bank (EIB) certainly plays a significant role. The European Investment Bank (EIB) is the bank

---

[6] Closed-end funds are mutual investment funds with a fixed number of participation units. In these kinds of funds, the right of reimbursement of the participants occurs only for predetermined dates. These features do not prevent the exchange of participants' shares on the market; however, fluctuations in their value do not affect the wealth of the fund itself because their redemption is predetermined. A typical characteristic of closed-end funds is, therefore, to have a long-term maturity, usually 10–15 years, and to have a higher entry amount than other funds. This set of peculiarities makes them a widely used instrument for investments in certain sectors.

[7] Circular Innovation Fund. More information is available at the link: https://circularinnovationfund.com.

[8] BGF Circular Economy. More information is available at the link: https://www.blackrock.com/americas-offshore/en/products/310165/blackrock-circular-economy.

of the European Union, and all of its members hold shares. Its activity is primarily centered on Europe, but it also supports European initiatives for international cooperation and development assistance. The EIB supports projects that contribute significantly to growth and employment in Europe, concentrating its action on the following priority sectors: innovation and human capital, access to financing by small and medium-sized enterprises, environment and climate change, and infrastructure. Fundraising takes place in the international capital markets through the issuance of bonds.

Specifically, the EIB has launched, together with the major banks and financial institutions of the European Union, a Joint Initiative specifically dedicated to the Circular Economy with the aim of investing at least 10 billion euros by 2023.[9]

In addition to the previously mentioned tools, traditional debt instruments (mortgages, loans, and credit lines) offered by banking actors and other financial institutions are also available. An example of this type of instrument is the Circular Economy Ceiling launched by Intesa Sanpaolo, a line of credit aimed at supporting businesses of any size wishing to invest in the transition and adopt circular strategies and business models.[10]

2.6 Crowdfunding as an Enabling Tool for Circular Transition in Companies

While the financial instruments employed by both public and private sectors to facilitate a company's transition are unquestionably important, they could be further supplemented by additional financing forms in a setting where diverse funding opportunities can aid in executing varied projects. For instance, as a result of the financial market crisis and the ensuing restrictions, small and medium-sized firms (SMEs) seeking financial aid through conventional financing channels like loans and bank credits currently face greater obstacles than they did a few years ago (Udell, 2020). Hence, securing such financial backing seems markedly more challenging.

---

[9] Joint Initiative on Circular Economy. More information is available at the link: https://www.eib.org/attachments/joint_initiative_on_circular_economy_en.pdf.

[10] Circular Economy Ceiling. More information is available at the link: https://group.intesasanpaolo.com/it/sostenibilita/supporto-ai-clienti-nella-transizione-esg/supporto-alla-circular-economy.

In light of this, crowdfunding can be viewed as a viable substitute for existing financing opportunities in the market, even when it comes to materializing circular economy projects by furnishing companies with the requisite financial resources.

As will be described in Chapter 3, crowdfunding can be used to support the realization of various types of projects, from those related to, for example, productive efficiency or the modification of traditional plants to use secondary raw materials, to those linked to the development of circular products. In this context, the potential of crowdfunding can vary greatly and contribute significantly to the circular transition, not exclusively as financial support.

The primary advantage of crowdfunding lies in its ability to secure capital. Crowdfunding can fill this vacuum during the early stages of startups, allowing small and medium-sized businesses to get the money they need for certain projects (Belleflamme et al., 2019). Some circular economy initiatives might be seen as niche endeavors or as having a strong regional emphasis. Because of this, crowdsourcing not only offers a way to raise money for startups and new businesses, but it also makes it possible to fund initiatives that might not be seen as profitable and hence find it difficult to get funding from traditional sources. Hence, crowdfunding not only enables the financing of projects that hold significance from environmental and economic standpoints but also aids in the realization of projects that face difficulties in securing funds via traditional channels. Consequently, crowdfunding can be characterized as an emerging offering in the financial services sector with regard to promoting circularity.

Looking at crowdfunding as a tool to create circular products, the potential does not stop only at the acquisition of capital. Among the potential of crowdfunding is also that of allowing the pre-sale of a product not yet completed for the market, thus acquiring the necessary financing to complete and perfect such a product (Hemer et al., 2011). This potential allows financing the fixed costs of production of a product before the start of the actual production phase. Also, referring to crowdfunding as a tool to create circular products, the support can also be marketing and, therefore, as a tool aimed at improving the corporate image by making it perceived as a company attentive to environmental issues. Crowdfunding does, in fact, heavily rely on social media and internet communication, which makes it much simpler to spread information about a project across geographical boundaries (Agrawal et al., 2015). For potential funders, promoting crowdfunding projects through online channels is remarkably effortless and significantly faster compared to offline methods that entail higher transaction costs. As financiers make financial contributions, they often exhibit a heightened level of engagement, thus allowing for the emergence of viral marketing effects through crowdfunding.

Another support for the development of circular products that crowdfunding can provide is that of market intelligence to understand how consumers will approach the product. Thanks to the opportunity that crowdfunding and platforms designed for this offer to ensure a rapid exchange of information with potential financiers, the tool also allows testing entrepreneurial ideas to understand their acceptability (Mollick, 2014). A case in point might be a product crafted from recycled materials, which may not be fully appreciated by consumers.

Lastly, crowdfunding also serves as a valuable tool in fostering co-creation within the realm of circular products. Numerous projects presented for financing on crowdfunding platforms receive feedback from funders. Such feedback encompasses a range of interactions, including queries regarding future products or services, concrete suggestions for enhancement, and even novel innovative ideas. In this regard, crowdfunding operates on the fundamental principle of co-creation, where customers or financiers are involved in the process of value creation.

References

Agrawal, A., Catalini, C., & Goldfarb, A. (2015). Crowdfunding: Geography, social networks, and the timing of investment decisions. *Journal of Economics & Management Strategy, 24*(2), 253–274.

Agyemang, M., Kusi-Sarpong, S., Khan, S. A., Mani, V., Rehman, S. T., & Kusi-Sarpong, H. (2019). Drivers and barriers to circular economy implementation: An explorative study in Pakistan's automobile industry. *Management Decision, 57*(4), 971–994.

Awan, U., Kanwal, N., & Bhutta, M. K. S. (2020). A literature analysis of definitions for a circular economy. *Logistics operations and management for recycling and reuse, 19–34.*

Belleflamme, P., Lambert, T., & Schwienbacher, A. (2019). *Crowdfunding dynamics.* https://www.econstor.eu/bitstream/10419/207188/1/cesifo1_w p7797.pdf. Accessed 11 January 2023.

Boulding, K. E. (1966). The economics of knowledge and the knowledge of economics. *The American Economic Review, 56*(1/2), 1–13.

Braungart, M., McDonough, W., & Bollinger, A. (2007). Cradle-to-cradle design: Creating healthy emissions–a strategy for eco-effective product and system design. *Journal of Cleaner Production, 15*(13–14), 1337–1348.

Cavazza, S. (2018). Storia politica e storia dell'ambiente in Italia, di Marco Armiero, Stefania Barca, Simona Colarizi, Simone Neri Serneri. *Ricerche Di Storia Politica, 21*(1), 63–74.

Chertow, M. R. (2000). Industrial symbiosis: Literature and taxonomy. *Annual Review of Energy and the Environment, 25*(1), 313–337.

Corvellec, H., Stowell, A. F., & Johansson, N. (2022). Critiques of the circular economy. *Journal of Industrial Ecology, 26*(2), 421–432.

De Jesus, A., & Mendonça, S. (2018). Lost in transition? Drivers and barriers in the eco-innovation road to the circular economy. *Ecological Economics, 145*, 75–89.

Ellen MacArthur Foundation. (2013). *Towards the circular economy. Economic and Business Rationale for an Accelerated Transition.* https://ellenmacarth urfoundation.org/towards-the-circular-economy-vol-1-an-economic-and-bus iness-rationale-for-an. Accessed 24 January 2023.

Ellen MacArthur Foundation. (2023). *Shaping a nature-positive future with the circular economy.* https://ellenmacarthurfoundation.org/topics/biodiversity/overview. Accessed 24 January 2023.

European Commission. (2015). The missing link—European Union action plan for the circular economy. Communication from the commission to the European parliament, the council, the European economic and social committee, and the committee of the regions, COM (2015) 614 final, Brussels.

Fraser, M., Haigh, L., & Soria, A. C. (2023). *The Circularity Gap Report 2023.*

Garner, A., & Keoleian, G. A. (1995). *Pollution prevention and industrial ecology.*

Geissdoerfer, M., Savaget, P., Bocken, N. M., & Hultink, E. J. (2017). The Circular Economy—A new sustainability paradigm? *Journal of cleaner production, 143*, 757–768.

Grafström, J., & Aasma, S. (2021). Breaking circular economy barriers. *Journal of Cleaner Production, 292*, 126002.

Ghisellini, P., Cialani, C., & Ulgiati, S. (2016). A review on circular economy: The expected transition to a balanced interplay of environmental and economic systems. *Journal of Cleaner Production, 114*, 11–32.

Haupt, M., Vadenbo, C., & Hellweg, S. (2017). Do we have the right performance indicators for the circular economy? Insight into the swiss waste management system. *Journal of Industrial Ecology, 21*, 615–627.

Hemer, J. (2011). *A snapshot on crowdfunding.* https://www.econstor.eu/bitstr eam/10419/52302/1/671522264.pdf. Accessed 4 January 2023.

Kinnunen, P. H. M., & Kaksonen, A. H. (2019). Towards circular economy in mining: Opportunities and bottlenecks for tailings valorization. *Journal of Cleaner Production, 228*, 153–160.

Kirchherr, J., Piscicelli, L., Bour, R., Kostense-Smit, E., Muller, J., Huibrechtse-Truijens, A., & Hekkert, M. (2018). Barriers to the circular economy: Evidence from the European Union (EU). *Ecological Economics, 150*, 264–272.

Kirchherr, J., Reike, D., & Hekkert, M. (2017). Conceptualizing the circular economy: An analysis of 114 definitions. *Resources Conservation & Recycling, 127*, 221–232.

Korhonen, J., Nuur, C., Feldmann, A., & Birkie, S. E. (2018). Circular economy as an essentially contested concept. *Journal of Cleaner Production, 175*, 544–552.

Lieder, M., & Rashid, A. (2016). Towards circular economy implementation: A comprehensive review in context of manufacturing industry. *Journal of Cleaner Production, 115*, 36–51.

Mangla, S. K., Luthra, S., Mishra, N., Singh, A., Rana, N. P., Dora, M., & Dwivedi, Y. (2018). Barriers to effective circular supply chain management in a developing country context. *Production Planning & Control, 29*(6), 551–569.

Masi, D., Kumar, V., Garza-Reyes, J. A., & Godsell, J. (2018). Towards a more circular economy: Exploring the awareness, practices, and barriers from a focal firm perspective. *Production Planning & Control, 29*(6), 539–550.

Milios, L., Christensen, L. H., McKinnon, D., Christensen, C., Rasch, M. K., & Eriksen, M. H. (2018). Plastic recycling in the Nordics: A value chain market analysis. *Waste Management, 76*, 180–189.

Mollick, E. (2014). The dynamics of crowdfunding: An exploratory study. *Journal of Business Venturing, 29*(1), 1–16.

Pearce, D. W., & Turner, R. K. (1990). *Economics of natural resources and the environment.* Harvester Wheatsheaf.

Preston, F. (2012). *A global redesign? Shaping the circular economy.* The Royal Institute of International Affairs.

Rizos, V., Behrens, A., Kafyeke, T., Hirschnitz-Garbers, M., & Ioannou, A. (2015). *The circular economy: Barriers and opportunities for SMEs.* CEPS Working Documents.

Stahel, W. R. (1982). The product life factor. *An inquiry into the nature of sustainable societies: The role of the private sector (Series: 1982 Mitchell Prize Papers), NARC,* 74–96.

Suárez-Eiroa, B., Fernández, E., Méndez-Martínez, G., & Soto-Oñate, D. (2019). Operational principles of circular economy for sustainable development: Linking theory and practice. *Journal of Cleaner Production, 214*, 952–961.

The World Bank. (2022). *Squaring the circle: Policies from Europe's circular economy transition.* https://www.worldbank.org/en/region/eca/publication/squaring-circle-europe-circular-economy-transition. Accessed 24 January 2023.

Tukker, A. (2015). Product services for a resource-efficient and circular economy–a review. *Journal of Cleaner Production, 97*, 76–91.

Tukker, A., & Tischner, U. (2006). Product-services as a research field: Past, present and future. Reflections from a decade of research. *Journal of Cleaner Production, 14*(17), 1552–1556.

Tura, N., Hanski, J., Ahola, T., Ståhle, M., Piiparinen, S., & Valkokari, P. (2019). Unlocking circular business: A framework of barriers and drivers. *Journal of Cleaner Production, 212*, 90–98.

Udell, G. F. (2020). SME access to finance and the global financial crisis. *Journal of Financial Management, Markets and Institutions, 8*(01), 2040003.

UNEP. (2022). *Emissions Gap Report 2022.* https://www.unep.org/resources/emissions-gap-report-2022. Accessed 2 January 2023.

Vanner, R., Bicket, M., Hudson, C., Withana, S., Ten Brink, P., Razzini, P., Van Dijl, E., Watkins, E., Hestin, M., Tan, A., & Guilcher, S. (2014). *Scoping study to identify potential circular economy actions, priority sectors, material flows and value chains.* Publications Office of the European Union. http://bookshop.europa.eu/en/scoping-study-to-identify-potential-circular-economy-actions-priority-sectors-material-flows-and-value-chains-pbKH01 14775/. Accessed 12 January 2023.

CHAPTER 3

Funding the Future of the Planet Through Crowdfunding

Abstract Digital communication technologies have significantly altered product creation and consumption paradigms, transforming end-users into co-designers and even entrepreneurs. In this context, crowdfunding, which emerged as a subset of crowdsourcing, enables individuals and organizations to fund projects through small contributions from many people, typically via online platforms. This chapter describes the fundamental aspects that govern crowdfunding and subsequently the various types of crowdfunding (i.e., Donation-based, Reward-based, Loan-based, and Equity crowdfunding). For each type of crowdfunding, examples of circular economy projects funded through these methods are highlighted, thus showcasing the potential of crowdfunding to drive sustainable development. The chapter concludes its analysis of crowdfunding by presenting one of the most recent evolutions in the sector: the advent of platforms exclusively specialized in supporting projects dedicated to social initiatives and environmental sustainability.

Keywords Crowdsourcing · Donation-based crowdfunding · Reward-based crowdfunding · Loan-based crowdfunding · Equity crowdfunding

---

© The Author(s), under exclusive license to Springer Nature Switzerland AG 2024
F. Corsini and M. Frey, *Crowdfunding for Environmental Sustainability and the Circular Economy*,
https://doi.org/10.1007/978-3-031-66211-9_3

37

3.1 THE ORIGINS OF CROWDFUNDING

Since the advent of the twenty-first century, the emergence of novel technologies has empowered corporations to adopt cutting-edge strategies and innovative business models where the consumer plays an increasingly pivotal and proactive role. Digital communication technologies have catalyzed a radical shift in product creation and consumption paradigms, altering the business strategies and models. No longer is the end-user merely the terminus of the value chain; they evolve into active participants, co-designing with corporations, offering innovative value generation methods, and occasionally even transforming into entrepreneurs by choosing to finance these endeavors.

In this landscape, crowdsourcing emerges as a prominent exemplar. This term embodies the outsourcing of tasks to an undefined collective, mediated through information technology (Blohm et al., 2013; Nevo & Kotlarsky, 2020). In its early days, crowdsourcing was seen as an instrument that could help corporations to spawn fresh concepts and innovations by integrating customer desires and requirements into the innovation trajectory (Howe, 2006), thereby harnessing collective intelligence (Surowiecki, 2004). Presently, in academic literature, crowdsourcing is comprehended as an innovation process that utilizes an array of specialized tools to produce substantial outcomes across a multitude of disciplines—from medical research to public service governance (Brabham, 2013).

Crowdfunding emerges as a significant subset of crowdsourcing (Howe, 2006). Although the definitions of crowdfunding are manifold (Table 3.1), its defining traits underscore it as a process where individuals or organizations endeavor to launch a specific project. This venture is bankrolled by funds raised from other individuals, typically via an internet platform.

Hence, a process of crowdfunding, employing digital platforms as brokers between entities like individuals, nascent ventures, or established corporations and prospective investors, facilitates the delegation of the capital gathering endeavor for the fruition of a project to the crowd.

Although crowdfunding is often identified as an innovative method for fundraising, there are numerous examples of how such an approach has been used before the advent of communication technologies.

An oft-referenced illustration of an early semblance to today's crowdfunding is the endeavor embarked upon to finish the building of the

3 FUNDING THE FUTURE OF THE PLANET THROUGH ... 39

Table 3.1 Definitions of crowdfunding

Definizione	Autore
"Crowdfunding involves an open call, mostly through the Internet, for the provision of financial resources either in the form of donation or in exchange for the future product or some form of reward to support initiatives for specific purposes."	Belleflamme et al. (2014, p. 3)
"The efforts by entrepreneurial individuals and groups—cultural, social, and for-profit—to fund their ventures by drawing on relatively small contributions from a relatively large number of individuals using the internet, without standard financial intermediaries."	Mollick (2014, p. 2)
"Crowdfunding can be defined as a collective effort of many individuals who network and pool their resources to support efforts initiated by other people or organizations. This is usually done via or with the help of the Internet. Individual projects and businesses are financed with small contributions from a large number of individuals, allowing innovators, entrepreneurs and business owners to utilize their social networks to raise capital."	De Buysere et al. (2012)
Crowdfunding is the "process by which capital is raised for a project, initiative or enterprise through the pooling of numerous or relatively small financial contributions or investments, via the internet."	Belt et al. (2012)
Crowdfunding "is an Internet-based funding method for the realization of an initiative through online distributed contributions and micro-sponsorships in the form of pledges of small monetary amounts by a large pool of people within a limited timeframe. It is the financing of a task, idea, or project by making an open call for funding, mainly through Web 2.0 technologies, so funders can donate, pre-purchase the product, lend, or invest based on their belief in an appeal, the promise of its founder, and/or the expectation of a return."	Hossain and Oparaocha (2017, p. 2020)

Source Authors' elaboration

Statue of Liberty's pedestal. Back in 1885, Joseph Pulitzer, who was at the time helming the New York periodical "World," entreated his compatriots for monetary aid to complete the statue's base. As a reciprocal gesture, he proffered the donors the prospect of seeing their names inked in his widely read paper. Within five months, Pulitzer managed to gather sufficient funds to accomplish the project. It is noteworthy that most of the initiative's participants donated only a dollar, yet the number of participants was so vast that it nonetheless resulted in a success (Harris, 1986).

The form of crowdfunding we are familiar with today seems to have entered the collective consciousness with the launch of some campaigns that have achieved incredible success in the early tens of the twenty-first century.

An example is the conception of the Pebble Smart Watch by Eric Migicovsky. Migicovsky realized he was persistently extracting his phone to peruse messages. He hypothesized a less intrusive method would be to have these communications surface on his wristwatch. Alongside a group of companions, Migicovsky created a rudimentary version of the watch, yet when trying to procure funds through conventional avenues, he found little success. In the year 2012, he elected to seek capital through the crowdfunding platform called Kickstarter. After approximately a month, Pebble amassed close to $10 million from almost 70,000 backers, hence becoming the most-funded project in the annals of Kickstarter at that point in time (Mollick & Robb, 2016).

A similar endeavor is the Veronica Mars movie, funded in 2013 via a crowdfunding platform. The brain behind the project, Rob Thomas, alongside star Kristen Bell, enlightened their fandom in a Kickstarter video in March 2013 that their aspiration of $2 million would enable them to craft a humble film. The month-long crowdfunding drive amassed $5.7 million, thereby earning the distinction of being the most monumental and successful film project in crowdfunding history at the time of its inception (Leibovitz Libedinsky et al., 2015).

Yet, the scope of crowdfunding transcends the bounds of creative sectors. Presently, it is a tool for sectors as diverse as journalism, local communities, and even academia. Indeed, in stark contrast to several other financing modes, crowdfunding endeavors exhibit a broad spectrum of objectives. Numerous such projects aim at collecting minor sums to kick-start specific ventures, such as an event, where the funds often come from acquaintances and family. However, more and more, crowdfunding is emerging as a feasible avenue for entrepreneurial seed capital, providing businesses with the initial resources necessary to set their new venture afloat.

Crowdfunding has attracted such immense interest in recent times that, as per certain technical analyses, the worldwide crowdfunding market in 2021 stood at an estimated $18 billion, projected to escalate to approximately $45 billion by 2028 (Vantage, 2021). These statistics are accompanied by the burgeoning of a multitude of platforms, exceeding 2,000 globally (Petruzzelli et al., 2019), each harnessing a variety of crowdfunding techniques across a wide range of product or service categories.

This proliferation of the phenomenon has consequently sparked academic interest, with a growing number of scholars delving into the subject, offering fresh perspectives in this nascent field of study and thereby generating an array of viewpoints.

3.2 Anatomy and Operation of Crowdfunding

In the functioning realm of crowdfunding, there are three pivotal roles: the initiator of the project, the crowdfunding platform, and the fund contributors. Figure 3.1 captures the interplay between these roles. Each party possesses distinct attributes, which are of considerable importance when endeavoring to outline the principles of crowdfunding. Drawn from these foundational principles, certain crowdfunding models can be extrapolated.

Subjects Initiating a Crowdfunding Project

Any individual or entity, either profit-driven or non-profit, seeking funds to bring a new product or service to life can embark on one of the many global crowdfunding platforms. In operational terms, a party with intentions to spark a crowdfunding campaign must select a suitable platform. Each platform has specific regulations surrounding campaign architecture, funding protocols, and legal factors tethered to the campaign (Belleflamme et al., 2014).

After having identified an apt platform, the project's creator will set in motion the campaign. During this process, the platform scrutinizes whether the project adheres to its stipulated rules before approving the

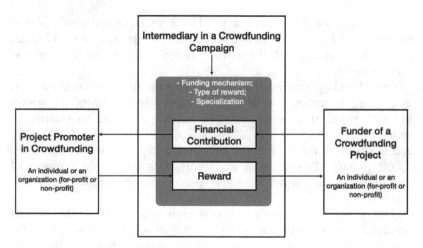

Fig. 3.1 Relationship between stakeholders in the crowdfunding process (*Source* Adapted from Haas et al., 2014)

campaign's launch. A shared attribute in several platforms is that prior to the campaign's beginning, project creators are bound to set a fundraising goal, in other terms, the financial target they aim to attain.

Finally, project creators must also curate a detailed presentation of their project for potential patrons, delivering precise data about the project, which includes its developmental trajectory and any linked potential risks.

The ultimate aspiration of crowdfunding project creators is to meet their funding objectives. Consequently, they must curate the information showcased (preferably with photos and videos) and offer updates about the project's evolution, both of which serve as evidence of the creators' intentions and help foster trust among the financiers.

Moreover, engaging with the financier community is deemed paramount for a crowdfunding campaign's successful culmination. In fact, being an active project creator and providing updates on the project's progression amplifies the chances of the campaign's triumph (Hobbs et al., 2016).

Considering a campaign centered around a circular economy project, a project initiator is required to pour substantial resources and time into elucidating the project's objective and highlighting its environmental importance, using suitable communication mediums such as visual aids, images, and well-crafted textual descriptions. For instance, encompasses all information concerning the type of materials utilized, impacts throughout the product's lifespan, potential environmental advancements over the existing standards, etc. A creator of such a project must be skilled at effectually interacting with potential financiers throughout the campaign, to transmit their readiness, and above all, the ethos attached to executing a circular-focused project (Petruzzelli et al., 2019).

Crowdfunding Platforms

Crowdfunding platforms operate as bridges between project initiators and prospective financiers. The role of these platforms can be illuminated using the theory of financial intermediation, a conceptual framework that clarifies the interplay and functions of intermediaries within financial exchanges. Financial intermediaries are cornerstone institutions in economic frameworks, playing a pivotal role in the savings-investment cycle; they supply capital, borrowed from capital providers, to other agents in need of capital, employing debt contracts for both parties (Gorton & Winton, 2003).

Capital suppliers experience differing potential yields based on the magnitude and nature of their initial investment. When scrutinized through the lens of financial intermediation theory, crowdfunding becomes more intelligible, offering a holistic view of the actors participating in campaigns and their reciprocal relationships.

In crowdfunding, agents in pursuit of and offering capital interact on the crowdfunding platform, which plays the intermediary role. Nevertheless, unlike conventional financial intermediaries, crowdfunding platforms do not partake in the actual financing process. They neither borrow, pool, nor lend money on their own behalf. Crowdfunding platforms merely provide certain functionalities and primarily act as entities that can facilitate relationships between project promoters and potential financiers by reducing informational asymmetries and minimizing transaction costs between these parties (Haas et al., 2014).

Generally, crowdfunding platforms conduct an initial screening of projects to admit them to the financing process. An excessive influx of promoted projects on a platform could decrease the probability of attracting funds, as these would be diluted over a multitude of projects (Corazzini et al., 2015). Therefore, an initial screening of the most promising projects and indexing the best projects on the homepage enable financiers to identify the most promising initiatives.

Key aspects to describe crowdfunding platforms refer to the financing mechanism, type of support/reward, and specialization.

The financing mechanism in crowdfunding platforms can vary from one platform to another. Generally, project promoters define the possible participation quotas and various levels of financial commitment. Each level of commitment implies a certain reward, which increases with the increase in the financed amount. The minimum contribution to partake in the project signifies the lowest monetary commitment that financiers can offer. The threshold of this sum exhibits a broad range; it can be modest, as seen in charitable endeavors, while it may escalate to thousands of euros when funding entrepreneurial ventures and startups (Mollick & Robb, 2016). In this context, most platforms operate under the "all or nothing" principle (Mollick & Robb, 2016). In line with this principle, project initiators receive the amassed funds only if they fulfill the predetermined funding target set at the campaign's inception. This is predicated on the belief that project promoters can carry out their project and deliver the pledged rewards only if they possess all the requisite resources. Nonetheless, certain crowdfunding platforms function under the "keep-it-all" principle, where project initiators receive whatever amount is gathered. This financing principle is especially employed for charitable projects or those that leverage crowdfunding as an auxiliary funding source (Cumming et al., 2020).

Platforms also differ based on the type of reward that promoters can offer their financiers. Specifically, platforms can support project promoters in offering a wide range of possible rewards, such as:

1. No reward: the financier donates to support the project without receiving any reward.
2. Pre-sale of a product: the financier's support equates to a prepayment for a product before it officially enters the marketplace.
3. Interests: the financier partakes in a loan arrangement.
4. Participation shares: the financier acquires equity shares in the project, such as in the establishment of a startup.

The risk level of capital contribution and consequent returns ascends from donation, through pre-sale, loan, and finally to equity, as illustrated in Fig. 3.2.

The final facet in the characterization of a platform is its area of specialization. By curtailing transactional expenditures and information discrepancies, crowdfunding platforms are able to amass resources for a broad spectrum of niche projects, which otherwise might grapple with limited access to conventional funding conduits. Additionally, crowdfunding platforms facilitate funding for projects with minimal financial needs, which are unable to access conventional credit markets due to their low profitability.

In response to these vastly diverse demands, crowdfunding presents a remarkable degree of specialization. This has engendered the rise of several niche platforms in recent years, each catering to a particular segment within the crowdfunding marketplace. The specialization of crowdfunding platforms has led to the creation of entities specialized in fundraising for certain market sectors, such as real estate crowdfunding,

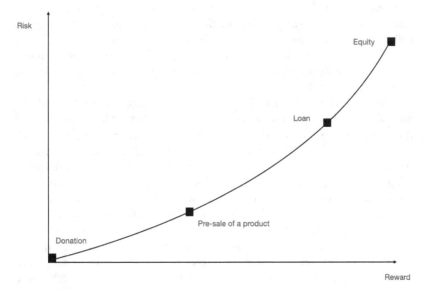

Fig. 3.2 Risk-reward relationship in relation to reward types (*Source* Adapted from Hemer et al., 2011)

all the way to platforms exclusively supporting projects dedicated to social initiatives and environmental sustainability.

Taking these aspects into account, for initiatives directed toward circularity, the role of crowdfunding platforms is indispensable for their success. Circularity-focused campaigns (such as those discussed in the subsequent subchapters) launched on platforms that spotlight such projects on their landing page, recurrently endorse them to prospective financiers, or even dedicate particular sections of their website for this genre of projects, stand a higher chance of success (Corsini & Frey, 2021). Another aspect of significant importance that could be one of the goals of crowdfunding platforms is to screen a project's sustainability characteristics alongside the screening done to admit the project to the platform. This could lead to the rejection of some projects that self-define as circular but ultimately are not.

The Financiers of a Crowdfunding Campaign

The last entity to describe is the financiers. Financiers partake in and fund a campaign propelled by diverse motivations, chiefly to glean material or financial gains, or when they harbor the conviction that their contribution will meaningfully bolster the project's success (Kuppuswamy & Bayus, 2017). Within the landscape of crowdfunding, financiers are privy to and mindful of the decisions made by their counterparts, and their actions are swayed by such behaviors.

The reasons for financiers to support a project extend beyond the prospect of obtaining material or financial rewards. Financiers may be driven to back projects owing to emotional connections, such as bonds of friendship or familiarity with the proposer (Gallemore et al., 2019). Another motive underscored in crowdfunding literature is regional identification. Often, a compelling reason for financing crowdfunding projects resides in the geographical closeness between the project initiator and the financier (Lin et al., 2013). Alongside geographical proximity, cultural affinity can also spur financial support for a project. It's observed that as the cultural gap between financiers and project proposers widens, the inclination to finance decreases (Burtch et al., 2013). For both geographical and cultural motivations, the rationale lies in the proposer's social networks, which are harnessed to boost the campaign's success. Additional authors emphasize the significance of the need for recognition. Fundamentally, the pursuit of recognition is a cardinal human need as it furnishes individuals with a sense of self-worth. In certain communities, such as open-source software development circles, users anticipate positive feedback from fellow participants and take pride when their contributions are acknowledged as substantial. Applying this reasoning to crowdfunding, financiers' names are published on the pages of the campaigns they fund. Having their name on a campaign page is sometimes perceived as an opportunity for recognition (Bretschneider et al., 2014).

Ultimately, financiers may also underwrite a campaign to confer social benefits upon a community or specific individuals, as seen in donation-centric crowdfunding campaigns (Salido-Andres et al., 2021). The role of financiers in a crowdfunding campaign transcends mere financial contributions to the project.

Financiers who find the campaign appealing may also help to spread the word to others in their social networks, thereby positively influencing the campaign's outcome. Financiers can also engage with the crowdfunding campaign and the proposer; for example, by offering ideas on how to enhance certain aspects of the project or suggesting functional changes (Corsini et al., 2024). In this context, many crowdfunding projects have benefited from the feedback of financiers, who also assume the role of co-creators, becoming an essential link in the value creation chain.

Specifically referring to crowdfunding campaigns focused on sustainability, and particularly on circularity, it is crucial to acknowledge the significant role of financiers. By choosing to support projects centered on environmental sustainability and the circular economy, individuals directly contribute to overcoming one of the primary barriers that companies face in adopting these kinds of initiatives. This involvement not only advances specific projects but also fosters a broader cultural shift toward sustainability. Through their financial contributions, investors play a pivotal role in advancing the goals of sustainable development, demonstrating that even small contributions can cumulate to create substantial global impacts.

With these aspects in mind, for campaigns geared toward circularity, financiers occupy a pivotal role, chiefly in propelling the campaign and the social benefits of their project through digital word-of-mouth channels, thereby enhancing the odds of success. Financiers deeply committed to issues of environmental sustainability can morph into ambassadors for these campaigns within their social networks. Indeed, capitalizing on close and pre-existing relationships, dedicated financiers can effectively convey positive sentiment and information to their networks, thereby fostering a shared trust around the initiator, the project, and its environmental benefits, consequently escalating the probability of the initiative's success (Petruzzelli et al., 2019).

In relation to campaigns related to circularity projects, financiers also have the role of interacting with the project promoters to suggest how to develop the project. The feedback can aid the project's development by highlighting issues and potential solutions but also help align the operational aspects of the project developed in the campaign with environmental sustainability goals or suggest environmental aspects to address in the development of a project.

3.3 Types of Crowdfunding and Examples of Circularity Campaigns

Crowdfunding can be broadly bifurcated into two categories: commercial and philanthropic; occasionally, certain projects may straddle both classifications (Fig. 3.3). In commercial endeavors, financiers anticipate some form of return on their investment, while in philanthropic ventures, funders do not foresee any personal gains. The subsequent sections explore the varied types of crowdfunding in detail.

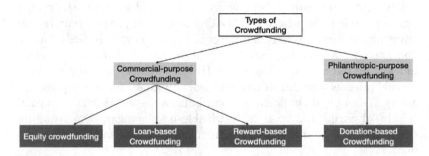

Fig. 3.3 Types of crowdfunding (*Source* Authors' elaboration)

Donation-Based Crowdfunding

Donation-based crowdfunding represents the most elementary form of crowdfunding. In this paradigm, funders contribute purely for philanthropic objectives (Salido-Andres et al., 2021). These donations typically bolster social or environmental initiatives, and the funders do not envision a return on their contribution. Generally, funders donate toward a cause that resonates with them, for instance, financing a beach cleanup drive. In some cases, funders may receive a symbolic contribution from the promoter, such as a message of gratitude, or the chance to participate in an event, course, or other activity; however, there is no material or economic reward in this model.

The promoters of campaigns of this type are mainly non-profit organizations, though in some cases, they can also be initiated by profit-oriented businesses.

The risk tethered to donation-based crowdfunding is decidedly low, given that project promoters bear no commitment to furnish any reward, and likewise, financiers do not anticipate one.

Donation-based crowdfunding is a useful tool to finance environmental sustainability campaigns (e.g., park cleanup campaigns, tree planting campaigns, etc.) more than circularity; however, there are also examples of such campaigns, some of which are presented in Table 3.2.

Reward-Based Crowdfunding

Reward-based crowdfunding provides funders with a non-monetary return; for example, the campaign promoter grants funders the chance to obtain a product prior to its commercial launch and widespread availability (Chen, 2022). In this model, promoters beckon potential customers to pre-order their product, proffering it at a reduced price than its eventual market rate. Notably, in reward-based crowdfunding, the sum pledged by the funder is due instantly during the fundraising phase, whereas the product will be dispatched by the promoter at a subsequent date.

In this form of crowdfunding, funders can also contribute to the project by making small donations without asking for any reward in return. In no case can funders who support these initiatives receive interest on the invested capital or a share of the business profits.

Table 3.2 Examples of circularity projects financed through donation-based crowdfunding on various platforms

Promoter	Campaign objective	Supporters	Funding received	Platform	Circularity aspects of the project
CESVI (Foundation)	The CESVI Foundation has initiated a crowdfunding campaign aimed at bolstering ongoing endeavors in the realm of recovery and enhancement of end-of-life textile products, with the goal of establishing a circular supply chain	4	€ 117,263	Forfunding	Extension of the useful life of the products; Reduction of waste production
La Cordata (Cooperative)	The cooperative La Cordata has embarked on a crowdfunding campaign to create a communal space dedicated to fostering experiences of sharing, exchange, and collaboration. This initiative is tied to themes of reuse, repair, and recycling of objects. It provides free access to both tangible assets (space, furniture, and do-it-yourself tools) and intangible resources (digital connectivity, the skills and knowledge of citizens and volunteers, among others)	203	€ 9,282	Produzioni dal basso	Extension of the useful life of the products; Reduction of waste production

Source Authors' elaboration

Typically, at the moment of resource commitment, the funders lack complete knowledge of both the capabilities and skills of the campaign promoter, as well as the final characteristics of the product; nevertheless, the risks attached to these types of crowdfunding for funders are moderately low. In the worst-case scenario, the campaign proponent might not be able to deliver the proposed product, and thus the funders might not receive the anticipated reward.

In general, the funders of these crowdfunding initiatives are the individuals who can be defined as early adopters, those who want to be the first to experiment with a new technology, new materials, or new functionalities. Reward-based crowdfunding is a highly useful tool to also finance circularity projects; some examples of such projects financed through reward-based crowdfunding are presented in Table 3.3.

Loan-Based Crowdfunding

The loan-based model implicates a peer-to-peer loan (Bradford, 2012), fundamentally a loan "among equals," facilitated by a platform serving as an intermediary, circumventing the engagement of a banking entity. In this model, funders lend funds for a predetermined period, anticipating the return of their funds along with the associated interest. The loan-based model deviates from other crowdfunding models in that the exchange between the promoter and the funders is exclusively monetary. Loan-based crowdfunding is a fascinating tool for businesses that can access financing at a lower cost compared to traditional channels without providing collateral, and for investors who receive a return to compensate for the relatively high credit risk assumption compared to similar investments (Bradford, 2012).

In these models, it is generally the platform that considers the request, evaluating the borrower's credit risk; if it is acceptable and in line with the platform's risk categories, an interest rate appropriate to the risk is set. In this case, the risks can be identified as medium–high for the funders who risk losing the entire invested capital if the borrowers are unable to repay them.

In this case too, there are examples of loan-based crowdfunding aimed at financing circularity projects in businesses; some examples of such projects are gathered in Table 3.4.

Table 3.3 Examples of circularity projects financed through reward-based crowdfunding across various platforms

Promoter	Campaign objective	Supporters	Funding received	Platform	Circularity aspects of the project
ID. Eight (startup)	ID.EIGHT, through crowdfunding, has crafted athletic shoes using agri-food industry by-products such as apple peels, cores, pineapple leaves, and grape skins and stalks. These materials, sourced from national supply chains, undergo specialized treatment to mimic the performance characteristics of leather	320	€ 36,040	Kickstarter	Circular design; Use of by-products; Waste reduction
Recofunghi (company)	Recofunghi, also through crowdfunding, has introduced a kit to cultivate fresh mushrooms at home using coffee grounds. The company salvages coffee grounds from cafes, packages them in unique bags, and sows the mycelium, the fungal seed. This distinctive kit enables the growth of mushrooms in the comfort of one's home	165	8.000 €	Eppela	Circular design; Closure of the biological cycle, Waste reduction
LastObject (company)	LastObject, a company that leveraged crowdfunding, has developed LastSwab as an eco-friendly alternative to the commonplace cotton swab. Composed of traditional plastic and bioplastics, the product boasts a lifespan of up to a thousand uses, thus positioning it as a potential replacement for the standard disposable cotton swabs	30.280	1.015.000 €	Indiegogo	Circular design; Long-lasting product, Waste reduction

Source Authors' elaboration

Table 3.4 Examples of circularity projects financed through loan-based crowdfunding across various platforms

Promoter	Campaign objective	Supporters	Funding received	Platform	Circularity aspects of the project
Celtic Renewables (company)	Utilizing the loan, the company executed a project to repurpose by-products of whiskey production for the creation of biochemicals and biofuels	2404	€ 2,363,094	Crowdcube	Closing the loop, industrial symbiosis
SEA Soluzioni Eco-Ambientali	Through the loan, the company revamped the setup of their vehicles, outfitting them with sensors capable of relaying operational data. This advancement paves the way for the initiation of remote monitoring and management procedures for waste collection and transport operations	513	150.000€	Evenfi	Efficiency of waste management processes

Source Authors' elaboration

Equity Crowdfunding

Equity crowdfunding signifies a profit-sharing model between the campaign initiator and the financiers, with the latter anticipating a financial yield on their investment (Coakley & Lazos, 2021). In essence, through equity crowdfunding, an entrepreneur or aspiring entrepreneur tries to find financiers to invest money in exchange for a slice of the business's prospective profits.

According to a recent report by the OECD (2022), equity crowdfunding is a valid financial alternative to traditional credit instruments, gaining particular attention in Europe. This form of financing can be essential, for example, for startups and small and medium-sized businesses, which can raise capital at lower costs compared to traditional financing sources (OECD, 2022).

Clearly falling within the area of securities sales, equity crowdfunding represents a very particular model of crowdfunding that also requires ad-hoc regulations. In Europe and the United States, for example, specific regulations have been developed to regulate this crowdfunding activity (Cicchiello et al., 2021).

With the advancement of equity crowdfunding models, different applications have also emerged that are not strictly related to business financing. Real estate crowdfunding, for example, is a method where investors acquire ownership of a property through the purchase of real estate shares (Gray & Zhang, 2017).

The risks associated with these forms of crowdfunding are greater compared to those previously presented. Generally, the capital requested by the promoters is larger than in other forms of crowdfunding. In this context, funders must consider that several years may pass before the investment yields a return. There's also the risk of illiquidity, related to the difficulty of reselling the acquired title to another investor. Finally, there's the risk of business insolvency—it's not uncommon for projects proposed by small businesses or startups to fail.

In this case too, equity crowdfunding is an extremely useful tool for financing circularity projects in businesses; some examples of such projects are gathered in Table 3.5.

Table 3.5 Examples of circularity projects financed through equity crowdfunding across various platforms

Promoter	Campaign objective	Supporters	Funding received	Platform	Circularity aspects of the project
Eso Recycling (startup)	Eso Recycling is an innovative startup that has designed a unique circular economy model, focusing on the recycling of accessories and end-of-life sportswear. These items are transformed into secondary raw materials used in the manufacturing of street furniture and rubber objects	138	€ 281,275	Crowdfundme	Reduction of waste production; Adoption of circular materials
Northern Light Composites (startup)	The company has devised an innovative boat-building process reliant on a recyclable composite tailored for leisure boating. This methodology ensures end-of-life recycling through a thermoplastic matrix and the use of low-impact raw materials such as flax fiber and basalt	30	498.500 €	Ecomill	Reduction of waste production; Use of circular materials
Felfil (small business)	The company plans to initiate a filament extrusion process for 3D printers that repurposes printing waste, thereby reducing the demand for virgin raw materials	52	119.990 €	Mamacrowd	Reduction of virgin materials, Reduction of waste production

Source Authors' elaboration

3.4 Specialization in Crowdfunding Platforms for the Environment

As presented earlier, recent years have seen a specialization in crowdfunding platforms, with some recently developed platforms exclusively supporting projects dedicated to social initiatives and environmental sustainability (Wehnert & Beckmann, 2021).

Recently, some platforms have specialized in so-called civic crowdfunding, which is aimed at financing social and cultural projects for the benefit of specific communities. In this instance, the aim of these platforms is to amass funds for public undertakings, such as neighborhood rejuvenation initiatives, territorial and communal development, or ecological advancement projects. In this context, campaign participants, often citizens of the local communities where the projects are initiated, are involved as donors or funders and become an integral part of the decision-making process. These types of platforms operate according to various methods ranging from donation to loan.

Similar to civic crowdfunding, other platforms that have emerged in recent years have specialized in loans for pro-social projects, with objectives of social well-being, human development, and environmental sustainability. The platforms that host these types of projects primarily operate with the loan-based crowdfunding model, although in some cases there are examples of donation-based platforms. The platforms operating in this field conduct a preliminary screening of projects, evaluating them both according to traditional financial loan criteria and a predetermined set of pro-social criteria (Allison et al., 2015).

Finally, among specialized initiatives, we should also mention those of energy crowdfunding, whose main purpose is to host projects for energy efficiency, installation of renewable systems, or other energy transition projects. The model with which these platforms operate is either loan-based crowdfunding or they adopt the form of equity crowdfunding. Financial backers through these platforms have the opportunity to invest directly and without intermediaries with small amounts in energy projects, reaping an economic benefit.

References

Allison, T. H., Davis, B. C., Short, J. C., et al. (2015). Crowdfunding in a prosocial microlending environment: Examining the role of intrinsic versus extrinsic cues. *Entrepreneurship Theory and Practice, 39*(1), 53–73.

Belleflamme, P., Lambert, T., & Schwienbacher, A. (2014). Crowdfunding: Tapping the right crowd. *Journal of Business Venturing, 29*(5), 585–609.

Belt, B., Brummer, C., & Gorfine, D. (2012). *Crowdfunding: Maximizing the promise and minimizing the peril.* Milken Institute.

Blohm, I., Leimeister, J. M., & Krcmar, H. (2013). Crowdsourcing: How to benefit from (too) many great ideas. *MIS Quarterly Executive, 12*(4), 199–211.

Brabham, D. C. (2013). The four urban governance problem types suitable for crowdsourcing citizen participation. In *Citizen E-participation in urban governance: Crowdsourcing and collaborative creativity* (pp. 50–68). IGI-Global.

Bradford, C. S. (2012). Crowdfunding and the federal securities laws. *Columbia Business Law Review, 1.*

Bretschneider, U., Knaub, K., & Wieck, E. (2014). Motivations for crowdfunding: What drives the crowd to invest in start-ups? In *European Conference on Information Systems (ECIS)* (accepted for publication).

Burtch, G., Ghose, A., & Wattal, S. (2013). An empirical examination of the antecedents and consequences of contribution patterns in crowdfunded markets. *Information Systems Research, 24*(3), 499–519.

Chen, W. (2022). A systematic literature review of reward-based crowdfunding. *Developments in entrepreneurial finance and technology,* pp. 146–181.

Cicchiello, A. F., Pietronudo, M. C., Leone, D., & Caporuscio, A. (2021). Entrepreneurial dynamics and investor-oriented approaches for regulating the equity-based crowdfunding. *Journal of Entrepreneurship and Public Policy, 10*(2), 235–260.

Coakley, J., & Lazos, A. (2021). New developments in equity crowdfunding: A review. *Review of Corporate Finance, 1*(3–4), 341–405.

Corazzini, L., Cotton, C., & Valbonesi, P. (2015). Donor coordination in project funding: Evidence from a threshold public goods experiment. *Journal of Public Economics, 128,* 16–29.

Corsini, F., & Frey, M. (2021). Exploring the development of environmentally sustainable products through reward-based crowdfunding. *Electronic Commerce Research, 23*(2), 1–25.

Corsini, F., Appio, F. P., & Frey, M. (2024). Green crowdfunding: An empirical study of success factors. *IEEE Transactions on Engineering Management.*

Cumming, D. J., Leboeuf, G., & Schwienbacher, A. (2020). Crowdfunding models: Keep-it-all vs. all-or-nothing. *Financial Management, 49*(2), 331–360.

De Buysere, K., Gajda, O., Kleverlaan, R., Marom, D., & Klaes, M. (2012). A framework for European crowdfunding. *European crowdfunding network (ECN)*. Retrieved January 28, 2023, from https://eurocrowd.org/wp-con tent/uploads/2021/12/A-Framework-for-European-Crowdfunding.pdf

Gallemore, C., Nielsen, K. R., & Jespersen, K. (2019). The uneven geography of crowdfunding success: Spatial capital on Indiegogo. *Environment and Planning a: Economy and Space, 51*(6), 1389–1406.

Gorton, G., & Winton, A. (2003). Financial intermediation. In *Handbook of the economics of finance* (Vol. 1, pp. 431–552). Elsevier.

Gray, M., & Zhang, B. (2017). Crowdfunding: Understanding diversity. In R. Martin & J. Pollard (Eds.), *Handbook on the geographies of money and finance*. Edward Elgar Publishing.

Haas, P., Blohm, I., & Leimeister, J. M. (2014). *An empirical taxonomy of crowdfunding intermediaries*. Paper presented at the International Conference on Information Systems (ICIS), Auckland, New Zealand.

Harris, J. (1986). A statue for America: The first 100 years of the statue of liberty. New York: Simon & Schuster.

Hemer, J., Schneider, U., Dornbusch, F., Frey, S., Dütschke, E., & Bradke, C. (2011). Crowdfunding und andere Formen informeller Mikrofinanzierung in der Projekt-und Innovationsfinanzierung.

Hobbs, J., Grigore, G., & Molesworth, M. (2016). Success in the management of crowdfunding projects in the creative industries. *Internet Research, 26*(1), 146–166.

Hossain, M., & Oparaocha, G. O. (2017). Crowdfunding: Motives, definitions, typology and ethical challenges. *Entrepreneurship Research Journal, 7*(2).

Howe, J. (2006). *Crowdsourcing: A definition*. Retrieved January 21, 2023, from http://crowdsourcing.typepad.com/cs/2006/06/crowd

Kuppuswamy, V., & Bayus, B. L. (2017). Does my contribution to your crowdfunding project matter? *Journal of Business Venturing, 32*(1), 72–89.

Leibovitz Libedinsky, T., Roig Telo, A., & Sánchez Navarro, J. (2015). Up close and personal: Exploring the bonds between promoters and backers in audiovisual crowdfunded projects.

Lin, M., Prabhala, N. R., & Viswanathan, S. (2013). Judging borrowers by the company they keep: Friendship networks and information asymmetry in online peer-to-peer lending. *Management Science, 59*(1), 17–35.

Mollick, E. (2014). The dynamics of crowdfunding: An exploratory study. *Journal of business venturing, 29*(1), 1–16.

Mollick, E., & Robb, A. (2016). Democratizing innovation and capital access: The role of crowdfunding. *California Management Review, 58*(2), 72–87.

Nevo, D., & Kotlarsky, J. (2020). Crowdsourcing as a strategic IS sourcing phenomenon: Critical review and insights for future research. *The Journal of Strategic Information Systems, 29*(4), 101593.

OECD. (2022). *Financing SMEs and entrepreneurs 2022: An OECD scoreboard.* OECD Publishing. https://doi.org/10.1787/e9073a0f-en. Accessed 24 January 2023.

Petruzzelli, A. M., Natalicchio, A., Panniello, U., & Roma, P. (2019). Understanding the crowdfunding phenomenon and its implications for sustainability. *Technological Forecasting and Social Change, 141,* 138–148.

Salido-Andres, N., Rey-Garcia, M., Alvarez-Gonzalez, L. I., & Vazquez-Casielles, R. (2021). Mapping the field of donation-based crowdfunding for charitable causes: Systematic review and conceptual framework. *VOLUNTAS: International Journal of Voluntary and Non-profit Organizations, 32,* 288–302.

Surowiecki, J. (2004). *The wisdom of crowds: Why the many are smarter than the few and how collective wisdom shapes business, economies, societies, and nations.* Doubleday Books.

Vantage. (2021). *Crowdfunding market—global industry assessment & forecast.* Retrieved January 28, 2023, from https://www.vantagemarketresearch.com/industry-report/crowdfunding-market-1484

Wehnert, P., & Beckmann, M. (2021). Crowdfunding for a sustainable future: A systematic literature review. *IEEE Transactions on Engineering Management.*

CHAPTER 4

Crowdfunding and Design for Circularity: The State of the Art and Relevant Examples

Abstract To move toward the paradigm of a circular economy, one of the enabling factors for businesses is the ability to conduct circular design of their products. The chapter begins with an overview of the various types of circular products and then, through an empirical analysis, examines how the tool of reward-based crowdfunding has been used to support circular design. In particular, projects developed in crowdfunding campaigns hosted on Kickstarter and Indiegogo from 2009 to 2020 are analyzed, showing the types of sustainable projects that have been developed and their success rates. The results show that crowdfunding has a still-limited influence on the expansion and market penetration of these products, but there is still a huge untapped potential for this instrument. The chapter concludes by proposing a series of managerial considerations for both companies and platforms to facilitate the easier utilization of this instrument.

Keywords Reward-based crowdfunding · Circular design · Circular materials · Long-lasting products · Efficient use products

© The Author(s), under exclusive license to Springer Nature Switzerland AG 2024
F. Corsini and M. Frey, *Crowdfunding for Environmental Sustainability and the Circular Economy*,
https://doi.org/10.1007/978-3-031-66211-9_4

61

4.1 The Concept of Design for Circularity

Conceived with sustainability in mind, "design for circularity" or "eco-design" embodies an acute awareness of a product's environmental implications spanning its entire lifespan. This notion represents a green supply chain initiative primarily internal to the organization, often taking place independently without significant collaboration with external entities such as suppliers or customers. The core objective of such circular design is to mitigate the environmental toll of a product throughout its life cycle—from procurement to manufacturing, use, and ultimately its end-of-life management. This ambition is pursued without relinquishing critical product parameters such as functionality, performance, quality, or other technical specifications. Therefore, through design for circularity, environmental aspects are integrated into the product realization process, considering all flows in the supply chain.

Design proves to be a pivotal phase in a product's life cycle where environmental performance can be significantly influenced. Indeed, during this phase, critical decisions are made on key product features, like the materials used, energy requirements, recyclability, and longevity, which ultimately dictate the product's environmental performance (Handfield et al., 2001). Figure 4.1 illustrates the lock-in of a product's environmental impacts in relation to the phases of its life cycle.

In Fig. 4.1, it becomes evident that a product's environmental impact is largely predetermined, accounting for 80%, during the design and development stage. Thus, if circular considerations are not adopted at this stage, the prospects for designing a product with reduced environmental impacts are rather limited. Designing for circularity applies equally to the development of new products and the redesign of existing ones. Therefore, the incorporation of a company's circular economy objectives during the design and development phase is crucial to extending product lifetimes, crafting them from circular or easily recyclable materials, and so on.

The complexity of considering circular aspects in the design process arises from the countless situations that may emerge within a company. Some companies indeed create, design, and produce their own products or services entirely on their own. Other companies, on the other hand, purchase components from various suppliers, assemble them, and then deliver them as the final solution to customers, thus solely designing the integration system of the components. Lastly, some companies outsource

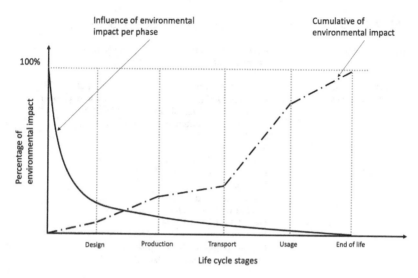

Fig. 4.1 Lock-in of a product's environmental impacts in relation to its life cycle phases (*Source* Adapted from Handfield et al., 2001)

product design and development to third parties. In this context, to ensure that circular considerations are addressed by designers within the design process, it is necessary that these are effectively communicated wherever the designers may be, inside or outside the company. Designing for circularity, after all, requires a team approach and the commitment and involvement of various internal corporate functions and, in some cases, also external stakeholders to successfully manage the various configurations mentioned above.

At the design level, there are several design options available to improve the circularity of products at different life cycle stages. Table 4.1 presents some of these options.

Products Made with Circular Materials

In Table 4.1, the first category of products designed for circularity refers to those made with circular materials. Mestre and Cooper (2017) suggest that a circular product should be made with materials having a low environmental impact. This implies that a product should be designed to favor the use of renewable raw materials, either natural or artificial.

64 F. CORSINI AND M. FREY

Table 4.1 Non-exhaustive table of approaches to design for circularity

Area of interest	Options for design improvement	References
Products Made from Circular Materials	Long-lasting Products	Bodar et al. (2018); Mestre and Cooper (2017); Shogren et al. (2019)
	Products Designed for Efficient Use (Including Installation, Maintenance, and Repair)	
	Products Designed for End-of-life Management	
	Design Improvement Options	
	Use of Recycled Materials Instead of Virgin Ones	
	Use of Biological Cycle Materials	
	Use of Artificially Renewable Materials (e.g., Steel, Glass, etc.)	
	Use of Used Components to Create New Products	
Long-lasting Products	Design of Long-lasting Products	Bocken et al. (2016); Guide (2000); Hazen eat al. (2017); Jayaraman (2006); Linton and Jayaraman (2005)
	Design of Products with Easily Accessible Spare Parts	
	Design of Easily Disassemblable Products	
	Design of Easily Repairable Products	
	Design of Modular Products	
	Design of Upgradable Products in their Functionality	
	Design of Adaptable and Reusable Products for Various Contexts and Situations	

(continued)

Table 4.1 (continued)

Area of interest	Options for design improvement	References
	Design of Products that can be Subjected to Regeneration Processes	
Products Designed for Efficient Use (Including Installation, Maintenance, and Repair)	Designing for Weight and Volume Reduction of the Product while Retaining its Functionality	Boks and McAloone (2009); Herring and Roy (2007); Söderholm and Tilton (2012)
	Designing for Energy Reduction during the Product Use Phase	
	Designing for Water Consumption Reduction during the Product Use Phase	
	Designing Products to Utilize Renewable Energy Sources	
	Designing Products that Utilize Minimal Materials throughout their Useful Life	
Products Designed for End-of-life Management	Designing Products for Easy Recycling	Clark et al. (2016); Geyer et al. (2016); McDonough and Braungart (2010); Vert et al. (2012)
	Designing Products for Easy Composting	
	Avoiding Design Aspects that Hinder Material Recycling	
	Designing Products to Avoid the Use of Biological Cycle Materials Together with Technical Cycle Materials	

Source Authors' elaboration

A naturally occurring renewable raw material can be defined as one that is derived from resources capable of naturally regenerating themselves within a short time scale, generally not exceeding a human lifespan (Harris et al., 2018). This definition excludes all non-renewable or fossil materials, like oil, which regenerate over millions of years. Natural renewable raw materials include materials such as cotton, wood, and bamboo.

Conversely, artificial renewable raw materials include all those derived from recycling processes. These materials are primarily those which can be recycled multiple times without losing their technical properties, and for which recycling chains are well-established. The two aforementioned conditions characterize artificial renewable raw materials as materials for which there is no resource loss along the recycling process value chain. Examples of these materials include glass, steel, and aluminum.

Materials that by definition cannot be considered circular include those hazardous to the environment and human health (for instance, lead, mercury, chrome, and cadmium) and critical raw materials. These latter materials are termed as such because they:

i. have significant economic importance for sectors like consumer electronics, automotive, aerospace, and defense;
ii. have a high supply risk due to high dependency on imports given these materials' high concentration in certain countries;
iii. lack substitute materials due to the unique properties these materials have for existing applications.

Examples include cobalt; vanadium; bauxite; fluorite. Therefore, designing for circularity should avoid the use of such materials (Bodar et al., 2018).

Long-Lasting Products

An alternate avenue to crafting circular products lies in engineering their longevity (Bocken et al., 2016). This process entails designing goods to linger in the economic system, preserving or amplifying their value throughout the full life cycle.

Products intended for enduring use are designed to be robust—capable of resisting wear without succumbing to breakage (Bocken et al., 2016). Moreover, products conceptualized to be adaptable and upgradable are also designed to have an extended lifespan. Designing for adaptability and upgrading prevents product obsolescence, ensuring it can be used for a long time by updating its value and performance, while simultaneously allowing it to adapt to changing user needs.

From a design perspective, prolonging a product's lifespan also includes designing a product with active prognostics, which allows predicting a product's future performance. These predictive tools can include monitoring usage conditions and can be a powerful impetus for predictive maintenance and support activities.

Moreover, designing a product for longevity also means designing it for "emotional durability," an approach aiming to counteract emotional obsolescence by creating long-lasting products that people will use for longer (Bakker & Hollander, 2013).

Long-lasting products are also designed to be repairable. Repair involves restoring damaged components to functional condition through replacement (Guide, 2000). The repair process usually requires fewer resources than producing a new item. An example could be the cosmetic repair of a product with minor external surface damage or imperfections like scratches, dents, cracks, and chips. The lower cost may also be associated with using still-functional components removed from other end-of-life products.

Long-lasting products are also those designed to be regenerable. The regeneration process differs substantially from that of repair; this process indeed aims to return products or components to useful life through repair operations and the replacement of outdated components that are updated. In this process, regenerated products/components typically have performance characteristics and quality standards equal to those of new ones. Concludingly, a product may also align with this category if it exhibits facile reusability, signifying that the entirety or portions of the product can be appropriated for alternate activities or applications (Hazen et al., 2017).

Efficient Use Products

A further category of circular products includes those designed for efficient usage throughout their lifespan. This approach to design enables the creation of a product that, during the user's phase of utilization, is capable of minimizing resource consumption.

Designing a product for efficient usage over its lifespan could, for example, involve developing a product that increases efficiency during usage by reducing the user's energy consumption (Herring & Roy, 2007). This approach is typically used for designing circular electrical and electronic equipment. Products bearing close resemblance to these are crafted to be energized by renewable energy sources such as solar or wind power, thereby possessing the potential to curtail the reliance on fossil fuels (Boks & McAloone, 2009). Reducing consumption throughout a product's lifespan can also apply to water usage; hence, products designed for this purpose are considered circular (Söderholm & Tilton, 2012).

Finally, a product fashioned to curtail the use of resources is also a product in which material stewardship is finely tuned. Products designed for this purpose can reduce the amount of consumable materials or additional components used throughout the product's life cycle (Söderholm & Tilton, 2012). Products that require substantial consumable materials for maintenance could be redesigned to use fewer resources, thereby also reducing waste production associated with their use.

Products Designed for End-of-Life Management

Another way to create a circular product is to design it to facilitate easy recycling of materials to manufacture new products, or to enable the reintegration of these materials back into the biosphere (McDonough & Braungart, 2010). Often, the design for end-of-life management is described in literature as design for "closing the loop" (Geyer et al., 2016).

Recyclable products consist of materials that, after a recycling process, can be reused in production processes. To be comprehensive, when talking about product recycling, it's necessary to distinguish between closed-loop and open-loop recycling.

Closed-loop recycling entails a system where every constituent of a product is recyclable, destined to create an identical product once more. An apt illustration of this phenomenon is the aluminum can, which, once recycled, can seamlessly transmogrify into new cans, barely causing any material degradation or waste production. It is self-evident that for products to be recyclable in a closed loop, their design should intrinsically cater to this objective from inception.

On the other hand, open-loop recycling signifies a recycling procedure where the recycled materials bifurcate into new raw materials and waste. As a rule, materials processed through open-loop recycling are repurposed. Thus, the feedstock for the recycling procedure transforms into a novel raw material, primed to serve as the basis for a distinct production process. Open-loop recycling could potentially lead to either upcycling or downcycling. A product can undergo an upcycling process, i.e., a recycling process that allows the use of the materials it's composed of in superior quality products and/or with greater functionality (Geyer et al., 2016). An example could be plastic packaging that undergoes recycling processes and the material obtained through this process is used to create a dress. Conversely, downcycling represents a methodology that transforms a product or constituent into substances of diminished quality. In this scenario, packaging which, following a recycling procedure, morphs into filler material. Despite the favored alternative being upcycling, this selection isn't invariably feasible.

Paralleling the notion of recyclable goods, certain products are created to effortlessly decompose or compost (Clark et al., 2016). These goods, derived from biological or organic substances, can be reabsorbed into the biosphere subsequent to their utilization. Biodegradable products are composed of materials that can decompose naturally through the action of microorganisms, fungi, and bacteria combined with sunlight or other natural atmospheric agents. This process should take place within six months, and the resulting elements can be absorbed into the soil as water, carbon dioxide, mineral salts, and other elements. Conversely, a product composed of materials that, after degradation, are transformed into compost is defined as compostable. Compost is a nutrient-rich substance commonly used as a fertilizer to enrich the soil. According to European regulation, for a product to be labeled compostable, it must be biodegradable within three months and must pass ecotoxicity tests as proof that it cannot have any negative effect on the environment (Vert et al., 2012).

Further Approaches to Circular Design

When talking about design for circularity, in some cases, the reference is also to the design of a product that allows the efficient production process of the product itself (Lim et al., 2022). In this case, the efficiency of the production process may concern the reduction of energy or water consumption (Bimpizas-Pinis et al., 2021). An extreme approach to design for circularity at the design stage is then designed for dematerialization, or the transformation of a physical product into a virtual product that does not require a manufacturing process.

Circular design can also concern the distribution phase of the product (Reh, 2013). Hence, circular design in this case allows for reducing the product weight or optimizing the product/packaging volume to reduce logistics impacts. Further Approaches to Circular Design are presented in Table 4.2.

Table 4.2 Non-exhaustive table of approaches to design for circularity of the production and logistics process

Area of interest	Options for design improvement	References
Design for Efficiency in the Production and Logistic Process	Design to Reduce Energy Consumption during the Production Process Design to Lower Water Usage during the Production Process Design to Minimize Process Waste (Hazardous and Non-Hazardous) Design to Utilize Materials Recovered or Recycled from Process Scraps Design for Dematerialization Design for Efficiency during the Product Transportation Phase Design to Decrease Necessary Packaging	Bimpizas-Pinis et al. (2021); Lim et al. (2022); Reh (2013)

Source Authors' elaboration

4.2   Insights on Circular Products Developed Through Crowdfunding Platforms

In order to understand how extensively the tool of crowdfunding has been employed to support the creation of circular products, it is feasible to scrutinize data gathered by specialized services that collect data from crowdfunding campaigns. For instance, Webrobots.io is one such service that allows access to the database of all the projects proposed for funding on the two primary crowdfunding platforms, namely Kickstarter and Indiegogo, dating back to 2009.

The data provides information such as the project title, a short descriptive overview, the initiation date, the terminal date for the funding, the category of the project, the country of the proponents, the count of campaign contributors, the sought amount and the sum amassed during the crowdfunding campaign, the ultimate status post-campaign (funded, canceled, or unfunded), and the project hyperlink (conducive for retrieving other pertinent specifics like the project description). In unison, the databases encapsulate upward of 200,000 projects for the span between 2009 and 2020 showcased on both platforms.

To pinpoint projects that are exclusively devoted to the development of circular products and to preclude, for instance, environmental advocacy campaigns, a preliminary assortment of projects was undertaken employing the classifications utilized by Kickstarter and Indigogo for project categorization. Indeed, both platforms sanction the classification of the proposed projects permitting creators to segment them into categories such as artist, dance, fashion, film and video, food, games, journalism, technology, and also campaigns endorsing societal causes.

Subsequently, a group of keywords, predicated on a review of the circular products literature delineated in the preceding paragraphs, were leveraged to isolate only those projects pertinent to the inquiry. Particularly, to identify campaigns focused on the development of circular products, the following keywords were used:

> "sustainable" OR "ecological" OR "organic" OR "recycled" OR "renewable" OR "durable" OR "repairable" OR "regenerative" OR "upgradable" OR "modular" OR "reusable" OR "disassemblable" OR "recyclable" OR "compostable" OR "biodegradable" OR "energy efficiency" OR "renewable energy."

In specificity, the research protocol was executed by hunting for these keywords within areas connected to the project title and its description. The employed selection process helped identify 3082 projects closely linked to the circular economy, dispersed across both platforms from 2009 to 2020. A modest quantity, representing just over 1% of the total projects promulgated on both platforms. Supplementary details pertaining to the chronological trend of these projects are illustrated in Fig. 4.2, revealing that out of the 3082 ventures, roughly 62% have been financed.

From the available data, it is also possible to determine the countries from which the projects hosted on both platforms originate. Individuals and companies from the United States and Europe, due in part to dynamics associated with the use of the two platforms and also due to heightened awareness of the issue, are those that have primarily resorted to this type of funding for the development of circular products, as seen in Fig. 4.3.

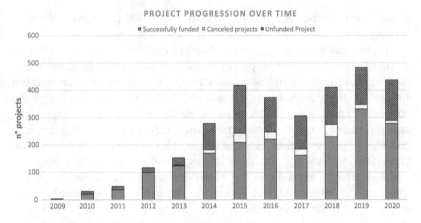

Fig. 4.2 Trends of projects for the development of circular products over time (*Source* Authors' elaboration)

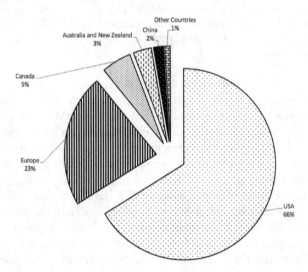

Fig. 4.3 Distribution of projects for the development of circular products by proponents' origin (*Source* Authors' elaboration)

Finally, using the previously described keywords, it is possible to have a distribution of projects aimed at developing a circular product for the period from 2009 to 2020 (Fig. 4.4).

From Fig. 4.4, it is evident that the majority of projects (37%) have aimed to develop long-lasting products (e.g., easily repairable, modular, etc.), 24% have aimed to create products with circular materials (for example, products made from recycled plastics), 9% of the projects have aimed to develop products that during their use, either use energy more efficiently or utilize renewable energy sources. Only a small portion has aimed to create products that are easily recyclable at the end of their life and compostable/biodegradable products. The same figure also shows that almost a third of the projects (precisely 27%) have generally defined it as sustainable or ecological. In regard to the latter point, it should be noted that neither of the two mentioned platforms conducts checks on the claims of the hosted projects. Within this milieu, it appears that numerous projects utilize the term "sustainable" primarily to lure

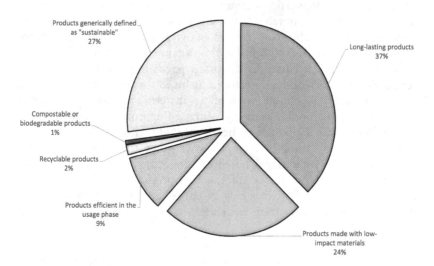

Fig. 4.4 Distribution of projects for the development of circular products by type of circular product (*Source* Authors' elaboration)

Table 4.3 Descriptive statistics of identified projects

Average amount requested in dollars in the crowdfunding campaign	Average amount raised by the campaign	Average number of campaign backers (n)
36.875 $	46.713 $	344

Source Authors' elaboration

eco-aware consumers, thereby indulging in greenwashing, or even that unethical promotional stratagem where products are depicted as environmentally benign when they are actually not. Table 4.3 delineates average statistics associated with the average sum solicited in dollars during the crowdfunding campaign, the average amount amassed from the campaign, and the average count of campaign contributors.

4.3 Examples of Crowdfunding Projects for the Development of Circular Products

Long-lasting products constitute the majority of crowdfunding campaigns. A noteworthy example of such a product, as depicted in this cluster, is a notebook designed for multiple uses, leveraging technology that enables the erasure of written pages via a microwave (Rocketbook, 2017). Additionally, the notebook is accompanied by an application crafted to transform written pages into digital notes. This repeatedly reusable product precludes the need for additional notebooks, thus diminishing the consumption of raw materials and the generation of waste. The crowdfunding campaign amassed approximately two million dollars in funding, supported by nearly 30,000 contributors.

Of course, it is not possible to assert that this product is more sustainable than a traditional notebook; indeed, to make such a claim, a Life Cycle Analysis (LCA)[1] of the two products would need to be conducted. Nevertheless, it serves as an exemplary illustration of how design for circularity, aimed at creating a product with an extended

---

[1] Life Cycle Assessment (LCA) is a systematic approach to evaluate the environmental impacts of a product or service throughout its entire life cycle, from raw material extraction to production, use, and disposal. This method aims to quantify the environmental burdens associated with all stages and identify opportunities for improvement.

lifespan, can be implemented. Another interesting aspect to observe in this campaign is that the product was not marketed as more sustainable than others; instead, the description solely references the product's technical performance. This represents a correct approach to communication that does not overemphasize potential superior environmental performances without having effectively measured them.

Another example of a long-lasting product is represented by a reusable cotton swab, which was also funded through a campaign on the Indiegogo platform (LastSwab, 2019). The product in question stands in contrast to traditional cotton swabs, which are disposable; thus, the project aims to address a significant issue related to such products, namely their abandonment in natural environments, leading to pollution.

Products crafted from what may be termed as low-impact materials constitute a substantial number of campaigns on reward-based crowdfunding platforms. An example of this type of campaign is ID.EIGHT (2020). The product in question is a sneaker constructed from waste materials of other industrial processes. Specifically, the sneakers in question are fashioned from three types of leather-like materials, which are derivatives of by-products from the food industry, including apple skins and cores, pineapple leaves, and waste from grapes such as the skin, seeds, and stalks.

4.4 A Deeper Investigation of the Projects for the Development of Circular Products

A more in-depth examination of the 3082 ventures was undertaken in a previous study by Corsini and Frey (2023). In this study, the identified projects were categorized using cluster analysis to gain deeper insights into how crowdfunding has been leveraged in the development of circular products. The following specific variables were used to group the projects into clusters:

- Number of campaign financiers who chose to support a certain project;
- Amount collected from the campaign;
- Amount targeted in the crowdfunding campaign;
- A variable assessing whether the crowdfunding campaigns were successful or not;

- Specificity of the keywords used to describe the product. To define this variable, a binary variable was constructed based on the identified keywords for project collection. This allowed for distinguishing between projects that used only generic keywords to describe their products (e.g., sustainable, ecological, or circular) and those that adopted more specific keywords (e.g., repairable, recyclable, reusable, etc.).

The authors identified five representative clusters, which represent different approaches and outcomes of crowdfunding projects in the circular economy. These were influenced by factors such as project quality, funding goals, and market demand.

The first cluster is characterized by a small fraction of unfunded projects that receive below-average support from both funding and backers. These projects set a higher than average funding goal. Corsini and Frey (2023) suggest that this cluster comprises first-time crowdfunders who may overestimate their chances of success due to media attention on successful campaigns, such as the Pebble smartwatch campaign which raised $10 million (Mollick & Robb, 2016).

The second cluster is characterized by a substantial portion of successfully funded projects with average contributions and backers. These projects request a slightly higher funding goal and use precise keywords. According to the authors, this aligns with environmental entrepreneurship categories described by Schaltegger (2002) and Petersen (2010), identifying them as "crowdfunding pioneers" capable of influencing other corporations to adopt circular practices.

The third cluster is characterized by a moderate proportion of funded projects with above-average funding and backers. These projects set average funding goals and use precise environmental terminology. The authors define these as "blockbuster projects," aligning with the definition provided by Liu et al. (2015). Such projects can have beneficial effects on related industries by validating the market and encouraging others to replicate their success.

The fourth cluster consists of successfully funded projects with slightly below-average support and funding goals. Mollick (2014) suggests that most successful projects on platforms like Kickstarter and Indiegogo are small, with modest fundraising needs. These projects use generic keywords and may capitalize on consumer interest in the circular economy.

Finally, Corsini and Frey (2021) identified a fifth cluster, which mostly includes underfunded projects with lower support and funding goals. Approximately 72.0% of these projects use specific terms to describe their projects. Mollick (2014) and Courtney et al. (2017) suggest that the lack of success may be attributed to low project quality, being in an early stage, or lack of market demand.

4.5 Conclusions

This chapter scrutinizes the role of crowdfunding platforms as financial tools aiding the creation of products intended for circularity. The results show that crowdfunding has a still-limited influence on the expansion and market penetration of these products, but there is still a huge untapped potential for this instrument. For easier utilization of this instrument, crowdfunding platforms could consider establishing a dedicated category for circular products. These project classifications, employed by Kickstarter and Indiegogo, serve to distribute projects among diverse sections, thereby bolstering their exposure to prospective backers. As it stands, projects seeking to finance circular products seem to be eclipsed by others, leading to their diminished visibility. For companies interested in developing circular products, it's noteworthy that new platforms designed specifically to host projects that can have a sustainable impact have emerged in recent years. Examples of these platforms include Oneplanetcrowd and TousNosProjets.

Another striking facet revealed by the data in this chapter is the lack of verification by either platform, Kickstarter or Indiegogo, regarding the assertions made by hosted projects. Numerous identified projects liberally employ the terms "sustainable" or "ecological," for instance, without any discernible basis. This aspect could profoundly influence project backers who, potentially attracted to the allure of supporting circular projects, might end up fostering projects that are anything but circular. In light of this situation, the platforms under analysis should concentrate their efforts on developing a uniform procedure to verify project claims.

For practitioners navigating this evolving landscape, understanding the conceptual underpinnings of circular design is crucial, as is applying these principles pragmatically. Entrepreneurs and companies should prioritize enhancing transparency, engaging effectively with potential backers, and demonstrating the tangible benefits of their products' circular design. In doing so, they bridge the gap between sustainable conceptualization and practical application, thus maximizing the potential of crowdfunding to support their initiatives.

REFERENCES

Bakker, C., & Hollander, M. D. (2013). Six design strategies for longer lasting products in circular economy. *The Guardian, 10.*

Bimpizas-Pinis, M., Bozhinovska, E., Genovese, A., Lowe, B., Pan-sera, M., Pinyol Alberich, J., & Ramezankhani, M. J. (2021). Is efficiency enough for circular economy? *Resources, Conservation and Recycling,* 167.

Bocken, N. M., De Pauw, I., Bakker, C., & Van Der Grinten, B. (2016). Product design and business model strategies for a circular economy. *Journal of Industrial and Production Engineering, 33*(5), 308–320.

Bodar, C., Spijker, J., Lijzen, J., Waaijers-van der Loop, S., Luit, R., Heugens, E., & Traas, T. (2018). Risk management of hazardous substances in a circular economy. *Journal of Environmental Management, 212,* 108–114.

Boks, C., & McAloone, T. C. (2009). Transitions in sustainable product design research. *International Journal of Product Development, 9*(4), 429–449.

Clark, J. H., Farmer, T. J., Herrero-Davila, L., & Sherwood, J. (2016). Circular economy design considerations for research and process development in the chemical sciences. *Green Chemistry, 18*(14), 3914–3934.

Corsini, F., & Frey, M. (2023). Exploring the development of environmentally sustainable products through reward-based crowdfunding. *Electronic Commerce Research, 23*(2), 1183–1207.

Courtney, C., Dutta, S., & Li, Y. (2017). Resolving information asymmetry: Signaling, endorsement, and crowdfunding success. *Entrepreneurship Theory and Practice, 41*(2), 265–290.

Geyer, R., Kuczenski, B., Zink, T., & Henderson, A. (2016). Common misconceptions about recycling. *Journal of Industrial Ecology, 20*(5), 1010–1017.

Guide, V. D. R., Jr. (2000). Production planning and control for remanufacturing: Industry practice and research needs. *Journal of Operations Management, 18*(4), 467–483.

Handfield, R. B., Melnyk, S. A., Calantone, R. J., & Curkovic, S. (2001). Integrating environmental concerns into the design process: The gap between theory and practice. *IEEE Transactions on Engineering Management, 48*(2), 189–208.

Harris, S., Staffas, L., Rydberg, T., & Eriksson, E. (2018). *Renewable materials in the circular economy.* Available at: https://www.diva-portal.org/smash/get/diva2:1549661/FULLTEXT01.pdf. Accessed on 23rd of November 2023.

Hazen, B. T., Mollenkopf, D. A., & Wang, Y. (2017). Remanufacturing for the circular economy: An examination of consumer switching behavior. *Business Strategy and the Environment, 26*(4), 451–464.

Herring, H., & Roy, R. (2007). Technological innovation, energy efficient design and the rebound effect. *Technovation, 27*(4), 194–203.

ID.EIGHT. (2020). Sneakers: Sustainable & cruelty-free from fruit waste. *Kickstarter*. Retrieved May 7, 2024, from https://www.kickstarter.com/projects/id-eight/sneakers-sustainable-and-cruelty-free-from-fruit-waste

Jayaraman, V. (2006). Production planning for closed-loop supply chains with product recovery and reuse: An analytical approach. *International Journal of Production Research, 44*(5), 981–998.

LastSwab. (2019). LastSwab—The reusable cotton swab. *Indiegogo*. Retrieved May 7, 2024, from https://www.indiegogo.com/projects/lastswab-the-reusable-cotton-swab

Lim, M. K., Lai, M., Wang, C., & Lee, Y. (2022). Circular economy to ensure operational production sustainability: A green-lean approach. *Sustainable Production and Consumption, 30*, 130–144.

Linton, J. D., & Jayaraman, V. (2005). A framework for identifying differences and similarities in the managerial competencies associated with different modes of product life extension. *International Journal of Production Research, 43*(9), 1637–1658.

Liu, J., Yang, L., Wang, Z., & Hahn, J. (2015). Winner takes all? The "blockbuster effect" in crowdfunding platforms. *Information Systems Research, 34*(3), 935–960.

McDonough, W., & Braungart, M. (2010). *Cradle to cradle: Remaking the way we make things*. North Point Press.

Mestre, A., & Cooper, T. (2017). Circular product design: A multiple loops life cycle design approach for the circular economy. *The Design Journal, 20*(sup1), S1620–S1635.

Mollick, E. (2014). The dynamics of crowdfunding: An exploratory study. *Journal of Business Venturing, 29*(1), 1–16.

Mollick, E., & Robb, A. (2016). Democratizing innovation and capital access: The role of crowdfunding. *California Management Review, 58*(2), 72–87.

Petersen, H. (2010). The competitive strategies of ecopreneurs: Striving for market leadership by promoting sustainability. *Making Ecopreneurs: Developing Sustainable Entrepreneurship, 2*, 223–236.

Reh, L. (2013). Process engineering in circular economy. *Particuology, 11*(2), 119–133.

Schaltegger, S. (2002). A framework for ecopreneurship. *Greener Management International, 2002*(38), 38–45.

Rocketbook. (2017). The Everlast Notebook by Rocketbook. Kickstarter. Retrieved May 7, 2024, from https://www.kickstarter.com/projects/rocket book/everlast

Shogren, R., Wood, D., Orts, W., & Glenn, G. (2019). Plant-based materials and transitioning to a circular economy. *Sustainable Production and Consumption, 19*, 194–215.

Söderholm, P., & Tilton, J. E. (2012). Material efficiency: An economic perspective. *Resources, Conservation and Recycling, 61*, 75–82.

Vert, M., Doi, Y., Hellwich, K., Hess, M., Hodge, P., Kubisa, P., Rinaudo, M., & Schué, F. (2012). Terminology for biorelated polymers and applications. *Pure and Applied Chemistry, 84*, 377–410.

CHAPTER 5

Success Factors in Sustainability and Circularity-Oriented Crowdfunding Campaigns

Abstract To fully understand how crowdfunding can successfully contribute to environmental sustainability and the circular economy, it is necessary to study and comprehend the success factors of sustainability-oriented crowdfunding campaigns. This chapter firstly analyzes recent scientific literature that sampled crowdfunding projects with both generalist and sustainability features to understand how the sustainability/circularity factor influenced success. Secondly, the chapter delves into the literature that examines potential success factors exclusively for projects dedicated to sustainable and circular initiatives. For conducting such analysis, the chapter reconstructs various theoretical frameworks from the relevant literature that have driven the analysis of success factors for crowdfunding campaigns explicitly aimed at sustainability and the circular economy. The analyses presented in this chapter serve as a foundation for understanding what has been explored in this domain and outline potential directions for future research.

Keywords Success factors · Literature review · Donation-based crowdfunding · Reward-based crowdfunding · Loan-based crowdfunding · Equity crowdfunding

© The Author(s), under exclusive license to Springer Nature Switzerland AG 2024
F. Corsini and M. Frey, *Crowdfunding for Environmental Sustainability and the Circular Economy*,
https://doi.org/10.1007/978-3-031-66211-9_5

5.1 Success Factors in Crowdfunding

A branch of scholarly inquiry that has drawn notable interest since crowdfunding's advent centers on the studies concerning the triumph of crowdfunding campaigns. Such research endeavors to identify diverse elements that could sway a campaign's successful outcome. Delving into this subject is crucial from both a theoretical standpoint and a pragmatic managerial view.

From a theoretical standpoint, such research endeavors to ascertain whether specific theoretical approaches hold true in contexts where new communication and information technologies, like those embodied by crowdfunding platforms, are employed.

In practical terms, the value of this research stems from gathering insights that can shape the crafting of crowdfunding campaigns and inform fundraisers' strategies. It can also impact the evolution of platform systems and services, illuminating novel methods for management and governance in settings shaped by web platforms with a multitude of stakeholders.

Research trends on success factors in crowdfunding campaigns have seen consistent growth in recent years, as illustrated in Fig. 5.1. Starting from 2015, there has been a rise in studies specifically examining success factors in crowdfunding campaigns aimed at supporting projects related to environmental sustainability and circularity themes.

The current literature indicates that success factors for crowdfunding can vary significantly depending on the type. The chapter first aims to describe the success factors for general crowdfunding campaigns, including those based on donations, rewards, lending, and equity. Subsequently, the chapter explores success factors specific to environmentally sustainable and circular economy-oriented campaigns.

Success Factors in Donation-Based Crowdfunding

The analysis of success factors in general donation-based crowdfunding campaigns is covered by a limited number of publications (e.g. Bukhari et al., 2020; Zhang et al., 2020). Such research emphasizes a positive correlation between the financial goal set in the campaign and its success, implying that campaigns requesting higher amounts tend to be more

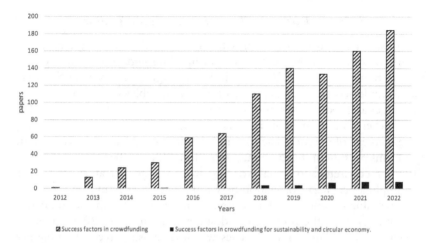

Fig. 5.1 Trend in research on success factors in crowdfunding campaigns over time (*Source* Authors' elaboration)

successful. Noteworthy campaigns requiring significant financial contributions appear to have a higher probability of success. In these cases, donors seem driven by the urge to contribute to a significant cause.

Some of these studies also highlight a positive relationship between physical and emotional proximity and campaign success, suggesting donors favorably react to campaigns that are geographically and ideologically closer to them. Research on donation-based crowdfunding factors (Lukk et al., 2018) reveals a positive correlation between affiliation with the education sector and the success of the crowdfunding initiative, demonstrating the perceived vital importance of education as a fundamental right by those contributing to crowdfunding campaigns.

Other determinants of success in donation-based campaigns have been pinpointed, such as the integration of a video, implying that multimedia tools lessen the cognitive strain during information assimilation, thereby promoting donations. Additional research points to a favorable link between the success of a campaign and the female identity of its advocate, as well as a direct relationship between the breadth of the social network and its triumph (Gorbatai & Nelson, 2015).

Success Factors in Reward-Based Crowdfunding

A substantial portion of existing scholarly works delves into the determinants of success in reward-based crowdfunding endeavors (Chan et al., 2018; Shneor & Vik, 2020). For these campaigns, a majority of the literature underscores the importance of various variables linked to campaign management, both in terms of project presentation and updates provided to backers and potential backers. These include campaign content, engagement of potential backers, and the timing aspects of the campaign. In terms of content, research indicates a favorable link between the utilization of concrete and exact wording in campaign narratives and their triumph; a beneficial correlation between the length of campaign text and its favorable outcome; and a positive connection between the frequency of updates from the promoter and success (Yuan et al., 2016). Collectively, these findings hint that cues which diminish perceived ambiguity play a pivotal role in achieving success.

Other highlighted factors emphasize a positive correlation between including a video and success, suggesting that, in this context too, reducing the cognitive effort needed to process campaign information boosts funding. Additional success factors include the perceived quality of the product and the perceived preparedness level of the individual or team promoting the crowdfunding campaign. These indicate that signals of the backer's commitment enhance campaign success (Chakraborty & Swinney, 2021). Intrinsically linked to the previously mentioned elements, several studies emphasize a beneficial relationship between the quantity of rewards presented and success, indicating that versatility and personalization in reward-centric crowdfunding campaigns resonate well with prospective supporters (Kunz et al., 2018).

Pertaining to the involvement of supporters and prospective contributors, research highlights a beneficial link between external endorsements and success; a favorable correlation between the volume of comments and inquiries and campaign triumph; and a positive tie between social media shares and success. These facets intimate that indicators of credibility and widespread interest amplify the achievements of reward-focused crowdfunding endeavors (Clauss et al., 2020).

In terms of temporal dynamics of campaign financing, research points to a favorable association between the funding status at the moment of inspection by potential contributors and success, and a positive link between early campaign funding activity and its eventual triumph.

Both insights allude to a bandwagon effect, wherein reaching a pivotal momentum can spur augmented funding as the campaign culminates (Wang & Yang, 2019).

In contrast to donation-based campaigns, for reward-based campaigns, the literature presents substantially inconsistent results regarding campaign duration. In some instances, studies reveal that campaign length negatively influences success, while other research reaches entirely opposite conclusions.

Success Factors in Equity Crowdfunding

The general literature that has examined the factors of equity crowdfunding is considerably narrower than that which has scrutinized reward-based crowdfunding (De Crescenzo et al., 2020; Ralcheva & Roosenboom, 2020). From these studies, primarily four factors emerge that influence success in equity crowdfunding campaigns. Among the determinants of success, some studies point to a beneficial link between the number of board members and the triumph of a campaign (Coakley et al., 2022). This suggests that human capital significantly augments the entrepreneurial journey. Another strand of research reveals a favorable correlation between the speed of fund accumulation in the initial moments and the campaign's success (Li et al., 2022). This insinuates that initial enthusiasm and financial commitments act as promising indicators for later investors, sparking a ripple effect of interest.

Further research delineates a positive tie between share valuations and the success of crowdfunding campaigns (Hornuf & Neuenkirch, 2017). This dimension emphasizes that campaigns with a too-elevated initial per capita investment request act as hallmarks of quality to potential backers.

One notable factor that detracts from the success of equity crowdfunding endeavors is the fraction of capital on offer (Drover et al., 2017). In other words, the smaller the capital share entrepreneurs are willing to correspond the greater is the crowdfunding initiative's success. In this instance, the willingness to give up a smaller capital stake seems to signal the entrepreneur's confidence in the initiative, proving rewarding in crowdfunding campaigns.

It's noteworthy that, in the context of equity crowdfunding, various factors analyzed in the literature have suggested insignificant effects on the likelihood of campaign success. For instance: company age, the presence of tax incentives for investments made, the total amount requested at the campaign's inception, and the investment's time horizon are all variables found to be insignificant in literary research.

Success Factors in Lending Crowdfunding

Among crowdfunding models, peer-to-peer lending has been widely discussed in the literature. In this case too, several variables have frequently been identified in scientific research as associated with success. Firstly, regarding variables tied to financiers, prior studies highlight a higher probability of success for projects displaying a superior credit score, essentially those suggesting lower risks for potential investors (Barasinska & Schäfer, 2014). Closely related to this variable is the debt/return ratio; here, research indicates a negative association with crowdfunding initiative success. This ratio indeed signals higher risks for potential investors (Kgoroeadira et al., 2019).

Other studies emphasize how the gender of the individual proposing the loan request and a previously successful loan collection can positively contribute to the initiative's success (Barasinska & Schäfer, 2014).

The scholarly realm reveals an inverse relationship between the fundraising goal and the likelihood of triumph in such crowdfunding endeavors (Ziegler & Shneor, 2020). This intimates that heftier financial objectives may telegraph heightened risks to potential backers. Diving deeper, other research accentuates the negative link between the span of an investment and its success; extended borrowing durations might echo a surge in risk and unpredictability for prospective investors (Bernardino & Santos, 2021). Predominantly, the research emphasizes a beneficial association between interest rates and success; elevated interest rates either hint at amplified profitability or act as a cushion against inherent risks for the investor (Barasinska & Schäfer, 2014).

In another vein, some studies advocate a favorable correlation between the interplay of prospective lenders and borrowers and the venture's probability of thriving; a reciprocated discourse can convey earnestness, clarity, and the borrower's dependability, bolstering the aura of trust (Cappa et al., 2021).

While an abundance of investigations delves into success catalysts in lending crowdfunding, a significant portion pivots around peer-to-peer consumer financing and altruistic lending endeavors. Few examples exist of research focusing on commercial and real estate loans. These less-studied crowdfunding areas could display results differing from those previously presented due to their closer resemblance to pure investment products, being more closely tied to companies' economic outcomes.

5.2 Do the Sustainability and Circularity Features of a Crowdfunding Project Impact the Likelihood of the Initiative's Success?

Much of the scientific research has endeavored to understand how the sustainability and circularity features of a crowdfunding project might or might not impact the success of the initiative. In this context, the studies in question sampled crowdfunding projects with generalist features and those with sustainability features. Those studies investigated how the sustainability/circularity factor influenced success. Through a literature review, 12 contributions were identified that aim to analyze generalist projects and sustainable/circular projects to determine how much sustainability might be a success factor. The studies identified and the results of these are contained in Table 5.1.

From Table 5.1, it's clear that a substantial portion of the research, precisely 8 out of 12, postulates that initiatives emphasizing environmental sustainability and/or circular economy principles bear a more favorable chance of succeeding than their general crowdfunding counterparts.

Delving deeper into these findings and the crowdfunding modalities scrutinized, a distinct pattern emerges. Within the realm of reward-based crowdfunding, a notable 6 out of 9 investigations champion the notion that endeavors rooted in environmental sustainability and/or circularity principles overshadow general projects in terms of potential success. Conversely, in the equity crowdfunding sphere, a mere half, or 2 out of 4 studies, resonate with the belief that such eco-centric projects surpass general ones in their likelihood of success.

Despite the limited data available, the discussed aspects seem to highlight how a project's sustainability/circularity features might be associated with increased success depending on the crowdfunding type. Few observations can be made regarding other types of crowdfunding given the presence of only two studies analyzing lending crowdfunding and none on donation-based crowdfunding.

Table 5.1 Research comparing the likelihood of success for projects with sustainability or circularity features with projects with generalist features

Authors	Type of crowdfunding analyzed	Platform	Sample of crowdfunding projects analyzed	Project reference year	Number of sustainability/ circularity-themed projects in the sample of projects analyzed	Type of data used for analysis	Analysis methodology	Results of the investigation
Hörisch (2015)	Reward-based crowdfunding	Indiegogo (international)	585	Published from June 15 to 22, 2014	10	Data available on the platform	Regression	No difference between sustainable and non-sustainable projects
Calic and Mosakowski (2016)	Reward-based crowdfunding	Kickstarter (international)	15,075	Published between April 2009 and July 2013	Not mentioned	Data available on the platform	Regression	Sustainable projects are more likely to succeed
Motylska-Kuzma (2018)	Reward-based crowdfunding and Equity crowdfunding	Polakpotrafi; Wspieram (Poland)	50	All those published from the launch of the platforms until July 2018	All projects were assessed for their sustainability	Data available on platforms	Correlation analysis	Sustainable projects are less likely to succeed
Lagazio and Querci (2018)	Reward-based crowdfunding	Indiegogo (international)	1507	Published between January 2014 and December 2015	40	Data available on the platform	Regression	Sustainable projects are less likely to succeed

Authors	Type of crowdfunding analyzed	Platform	Sample of crowdfunding projects analyzed	Project reference year	Number of sustainability/circularity-themed projects in the sample of projects analyzed	Type of data used for analysis	Analysis methodology	Results of the investigation
Vismara (2019)	Equity crowdfunding	Crowdcube (United Kingdom); Seedrs (United Kingdom)	345	Published between 2014 and 2015	124	Data available on platforms	Regression	No difference between sustainable and non-sustainable projects
Hörisch and Tenner (2020)	Loan-based crowdfunding and equity crowdfunding	Seedmatch (Germany), Companisto (Germany); First Democracy (United States); Start Engine (United States)	318	All those published from the launch of the platforms until April 18, 2018	All projects were assessed for their sustainability	Data available on platforms	Regression	Sustainable projects are more likely to succeed
Mastrangelo et al. (2020)	Reward-based crowdfunding	2 platforms (not mentioned)	53	Published between 2016 and 2018	Not mentioned	Questionnaire administered to project creators	Fuzzy Set Qualitative Comparative Analysis	Sustainable projects are more likely to succeed
Ljumović et al. (2021)	Reward-based crowdfunding	Kickstarter (international)	337	Published between 2009 and the first half of 2019	37	Data available on the platform	Regression	Sustainable projects are more likely to succeed
Chan et al. (2021)	Reward-based crowdfunding	Kickstarter (international)	81,765	Published between April 29, 2009 and May 6, 2013	3607	Data available on the platform	Regression	Sustainable projects are more likely to succeed

(continued)

Table 5.1 (continued)

Authors	Type of crowdfunding analyzed	Platform	Sample of crowdfunding projects analyzed	Project reference year	Number of sustainability/ circularity-themed projects in the sample of projects analyzed	Type of data used for analysis	Analysis methodology	Results of the investigation
Siebeneicher et al. (2022)	Loan-based crowdfunding and equity crowdfunding	4 Meta-platforms (investmentcheck.de, crowdinvest.de, crowdfunding.de, kritische-anleger) (Germany)	434	Published between 2016 and 2021	61	Data available on platforms	Regression	Sustainable projects are more likely to succeed
Siebeneicher and Bock (2022)	Reward-based crowdfunding	Kickstarter (international)	45,608	Published between 2009 and the end of 2019	Not mentioned	Data available on the platform	Regression	Sustainable projects are more likely to succeed
Dalla Chiesa et al. (2022)	Reward-based crowdfunding	Kickstarter (international)	283	Published between 17 October and 15 December 2017	69	Data available on the platform	Regression	Sustainable projects are more likely to succeed

Source Authors' elaboration

5.3 Factors of Success Discussed in Literature on Crowdfunding Campaigns Focused on Sustainability and Circularity

Academic literature on crowdfunding campaigns has also delved deep into what could be the success factors, exclusively examining projects dedicated to sustainable and circular initiatives. In this case, Table 5.2 lists the main research on the topic along with some details to better understand these studies (e.g., type of crowdfunding analyzed, sample of crowdfunding projects studied, theoretical framework used, etc.). The following sections detail both the theoretical frameworks that have driven the analysis of success factors for crowdfunding campaigns explicitly geared toward sustainability and the circular economy and those that have emerged as the primary success factors in these campaigns.

Factors of Success Analyzed in Literature: Theoretical Frameworks Motivating the Research

As shown in Table 5.2, there are various theoretical frameworks that have propelled the analysis of success factors for crowdfunding campaigns explicitly directed toward sustainability and circular economy. The following sections delve into some of these theoretical approaches.

Contract Failure Theory
Contractual failure is a specific aspect of the broader economic theory of "market failure," defining conditions where free competition among profit-seeking firms fails to efficiently deliver certain goods or services (Hansmann, 1980). Contract failure arises when consumers feel ill-equipped to competently judge the quality or quantity of services they receive (Hansmann, 1987). Under this circumstance, consumers might be hesitant to purchase the goods and services they need, fearing deception.

The primary source of contract failure is a condition termed "information asymmetry," wherein producers possess a more precise knowledge of the quantity, quality, and cost of services compared to consumers. Three main causes underlie information asymmetry. Firstly, some goods and services may inherently be complex or their quality hard to ascertain. The technical and multifaceted nature of medical care or higher education serves as an illustration. Secondly, the consumer might simply lack the ability to evaluate the services they receive. Childcare or services for

Table 5.2 Research on the likelihood of success for projects with sustainability or circularity features

Authors	Type of crowdfunding analyzed	Platform	Sample of crowdfunding projects analyzed	Reference year of projects	Type of data used for analysis	Analysis methodology	Theoretical framework used
Hörisch (2018)	Reward-based crowdfunding	Ecocrowd (international); Oneplanetcrowd (international)	58	Published before December 2015	Data available on platforms	Regression	Theory of contract failure; Rational choice theory
Bento et al. (2019)	Reward-based crowdfunding	Kickstarter (international)	869	Published between 2014 and 2017	Data available on the platform	Regression	Theory of self-determination
Rossolini et al. (2021)	Reward-based crowdfunding	Indiegogo (international)	86	Published between 2015 and 2020	Data available on the platform	Regression	Message framing theory
Kubo et al. (2021)	Reward- and donations-based crowdfunding	Readyfor (Japan)	473	Published between January 2013 and September 2019	Data available on the platform	Regression	–
Prędkiewicz et al. (2021)	Reward-based crowdfunding	11 different platforms	139	Published between April 2017 and August 2017	Data available on platforms	Regression	–

Authors	Type of crowdfunding analyzed	Platform	Sample of crowdfunding projects analyzed	Reference year of projects	Type of data used for analysis	Analysis methodology	Theoretical framework used
Corsini and Frey (2021)	Reward-based crowdfunding	Kickstarter (international); Indiegogo (international)	3082	Published between 2009 and 2020	Data available on platforms	Regression	Theory of information diagnostics
Berns et al. (2022)	Reward-based crowdfunding	Kickstarter (international)	113	Published between 2013 and 2018	Data available on the platform	Regression	Theory of legitimacy
Caputo et al. (2022)	Equity crowdfunding	6 Italian platforms	33	Published between 2014 and 2020	Data available on platforms	Fuzzy Set Qualitative Comparative Analysis	Theory of legitimacy, theory of collective action
Behrendt et al. (2022)	All four types	Not specified	6	Published between 2018 and 2019	Questionnaire and investor interviews	Multiple Case Study	Principles of proximity
Zhang et al. (2022)	Reward-based crowdfunding	Not specified	Not specified	Not specified	Questionnaire and investor interviews	Analytic hierarchy process	–

(continued)

Table 5.2 (continued)

Authors	Type of crowdfunding analyzed	Platform	Sample of crowdfunding projects analyzed	Reference year of projects	Type of data used for analysis	Analysis methodology	Theoretical framework used
Otte and Maehle (2022)	Reward-based crowdfunding	Kickstarter (international)	38	Not specified	Data available on the platform	Qualitative Comparative Analysis	
Corsini and Frey (2023)	Reward-based crowdfunding	Kickstarter (international); Indiegogo (international)	113	Published between 2009 and 2020	Questionnaire administered to project creators	Regression	–

Source Authors' elaboration

the mentally ill or elderly disabled exemplify this. Thirdly, some services may be purchased by an individual different from the end consumer. In such cases, the buyer doesn't directly experience the service and might struggle to obtain reliable information from the consumer.

One or more of these conditions might characterize a particular service, leading to contract failures that hinder the smooth operation of typical markets due to consumers fearing potential exploitation (Hansmann, 1987).

This theory has been applied in crowdfunding research, especially concerning campaigns explicitly directed toward environmental sustainability and the circular economy. As with many situations involving contract failure, backers might face challenges in assessing the quality of the project, product, or organization they are investing in through the crowdfunding campaign. In crowdfunding campaigns, backers cannot thoroughly inspect the project or organization but must rely on the limited information provided by the project or organization's creator. This can induce an information asymmetry between backers and creators, where creators have a more accurate understanding of the project or organization's conditions and possibilities than backers do (Belleflamme et al., 2014). Moreover, in reward-based crowdfunding, buying goods and services that don't exist yet or haven't been produced implies that backers can't judge the product or service's quality before funding. This can further challenge backers when deciding whether to invest in a project.

Legitimacy Theory

Another theoretical approach used in crowdfunding research, especially with respect to campaigns specifically aimed at sustainability and the circular economy, is the legitimacy theory.

Suchman (1995) posits that legitimacy is conceived as the belief or presumption that an entity's endeavors are worthy, proper, or fitting within a tapestry of societal norms, values, convictions, and interpretations. At its core, legitimacy serves as a conduit assisting organizations in championing voluntary ecological and societal undertakings, honoring the societal covenant, and securing affirmation of their ambitions.

Social perceptions about an organization's activities are tied to societal expectations; when these defy moral values, the organization can face severe restrictions, even to the point of collapse (Suchman, 1995). In this context, an organization must justify its existence through legitimate actions that don't endanger society or the environment it operates within.

The literature on legitimacy implies an organization's survival hinges on its legitimization processes and how it manages ongoing societal pressures and challenges. The purpose of legitimization processes is to earn and maintain stakeholder approval. The legitimacy theory boasts a rich disciplinary background, grounded in institutional theory (Scott, 1987) and stakeholder theory (Freeman, 1984). More generally, the legitimacy theory builds upon the managerial heritage that connects traditional norms and values with modern ethics.

Legitimacy theory has been used as a theoretical backbone in crowdfunding research, particularly regarding campaigns explicitly geared toward environmental sustainability and the circular economy for various reasons. Firstly, crowdfunding is premised on the idea of involving a community of individuals and creating a collective action to achieve a mutual goal. In this light, a crowdfunding initiative's legitimacy hinges on the community's perception that the presented project deserves support and funding. Environmental sustainability or circularity aspects in this context might serve as legitimacy tools for the individual proposing the project through a crowdfunding campaign, potentially yielding positive outcomes for the campaign.

The legitimacy theory also illuminates how crowdfunding campaigns attempt to gain legitimacy by presenting information and forging relations with stakeholders. For instance, a crowdfunding campaign might strive to enhance its legitimacy by providing detailed information about the project, its objectives, and its management. This way, the crowdfunding campaign can bolster its credibility and its ability to attract backers.

Lastly, the legitimacy theory is used to understand backers' roles in supporting a crowdfunding project. Backers can evaluate a project's legitimacy based on their expectations, values, and beliefs. In this sense, crowdfunding becomes a shared legitimacy-building process, wherein the project-presenting organization and backers collaborate to foster a legitimate, socially or environmentally sustainable collective action.

Collective Action Theory

Another theoretical approach employed is the collective action theory. Collective actions refer to those initiated by two or more people to pursue a common good, termed a "public good" (Marwell & Oliver, 1993). Such goods are non-excludable, implying anyone can benefit from the good regardless of their contribution to its creation, and non-rivalrous, meaning their consumption doesn't reduce their availability to others (Chamberlin, 1974). Public goods vary from traditional physical assets like parks and bridges to political goods like public policies, and intangible assets like information system databases.

Collective actions leading to public goods creation hold unique theoretical interests, setting them apart from the solo actions of a resource-rich individual contributor. Central tenets of the traditional collective action theory are the "free riding" dilemma (Hardin, 1982). Free riding arises when potential contributors weigh whether to contribute to a public good or merely benefit once others have established it. This problem is acute in the initial stages of public good creation, as early contributors gain limited immediate benefits. As a result, the incentive structure leads each participant to wait for others to contribute first. Hence, the public good isn't created unless there are keen, resource-rich participants willing to bear significant upfront costs without direct corresponding benefits.

Research grounded in this theory emphasizes that many barriers to collective action are communal and organizational, like pinpointing and engaging suitable participants, motivating private resource allocation, persuading sustained engagement despite short-term setbacks and long-term risks, and efficient effort coordination. Therefore, reliance on organization lies at the heart of the original collective action theory (Olson, 1965).

The collective action theory is used in crowdfunding research, and also those studies exploring campaigns explicitly geared toward environmental sustainability and the circular economy. This is because crowdfunding is a collaborative funding form, involving numerous individuals backing a project or idea. Scholars have utilized collective action theory to probe factors influencing individual participation in crowdfunding campaigns and emergent group dynamics. For instance, this theory has been leveraged to examine the roles of individual motivation, group belongingness, mutual trust, and social resonance effect in shaping individual participation in sustainability or circular-focused crowdfunding campaigns (Caputo et al., 2022).

Self-Determination Theory
The self-determination theory stands as a notable framework for delving into the intricacies of human motivation (Deci, 1971). It stands apart

from many theories that view motivation as a monolithic concept, distinguishing motivation into autonomous and controlled forms (Deci & Ryan, 2008). Research into intrinsic and extrinsic reward effects on human motivation (Deci & Ryan, 1980) suggests that external incentives, like monetary rewards for puzzle-solving, can dampen intrinsic motivation for the task (Deci, 1971). Conversely, receiving positive feedback on skill application during an activity can boost participants' intrinsic motivation. Such insights prompted further exploration of motivation from a qualitative angle (Deci & Ryan, 2008).

As per the self-determination theory, intrinsic drive arises from one's fundamental psychological desires (Ryan & Deci, 2000). The influence of external rewards on this innate drive is discerned through the lens of perceived personal causality and the satisfaction of these elemental psychological necessities (Ryan & Deci, 2000). Essential psychological yearnings such as autonomy, proficiency, and a sense of connection are crucial to nurturing intrinsic motivation (Deci & Ryan, 2008). Furthermore, how one perceives the causality of their actions profoundly molds the essence of their intrinsic drive (Ryan & Deci, 2000). The self-determination theory has profoundly informed our grasp of human motivation across domains, including psychology, education, and sports. For example, it's been harnessed to explore student motivation in schools (Ryan & Deci, 2000) and athletes in sports (Reinboth & Duda, 2006). It's also been applied to discern well-being facets, like mental health (Deci & Ryan, 2008) and life quality (Sheldon & Niemiec, 2006).

Within the scope of crowdfunding research, particularly those campaigns underscored by environmental sustainability and the circular economy, the self-determination theory sheds light on patron behaviors. This theory provides a robust foundation to discern the role of intrinsic motivation when deciding to endorse a crowdfunding endeavor. Research in this domain (for instance, Chen et al., 2021) posits that intrinsic motivation augments patrons' inclination to support, amplifying their intention to contribute financially. Notably, autonomy emerges as a pivotal determinant in the choice to support a project, eclipsing extrinsic motivations. Further investigations underscore a harmonious link between intrinsic motivation and patron contentment, insinuating that monetary contributions in crowdfunding can bestow innate rewards (Zhang et al., 2017). In this context, the self-determination theory aids in decoding crowdfunding backers' behavior, spotlighting the centrality of autonomous motivation in project support. The cited research examples underscore autonomy and satisfaction as decisive factors in crowdfunding backers' decision-making process.

Rational Choice Theory
The rational choice theory underscores the rational decisions individuals tend to make in diverse situations of choice (see for instance: Smith 1776; Witztum, 2005). This theory suggests that people aim to optimize their benefits, whether they be economic, social, or psychological in nature (Becker, 1976). While primarily crafted by economists, this theory has permeated into domains such as psychology, sociology, and politics.

A cornerstone of the rational choice theory is the concept of utility. It suggests that individuals seek to maximize their utility, the benefit derived from a particular choice. While often quantified in monetary terms, the utility can also measure happiness, satisfaction, or psychological well-being, and its perception may differ among individuals and situations (Kahneman & Tversky, 1979).

Another key element is the concept of expectations. Individuals base decisions on their predictions about future outcomes, drawing from past and present information or future forecasts. Again, these expectations can be subjective, rooted in one's personal perceptions.

Economics is a major domain employing the rational choice theory (Varian, 1992). For instance, it's used to scrutinize consumer choices, assuming individuals select goods and services based on preferences and prices. Similarly, in business research, it supports the notion that companies choose productive factors to maximize profits, underlining the presumption that individuals make rational choices considering their perceived advantages.

Despite its theoretical prominence in fields like psychology and sociology, the rational choice theory faces criticism (Coleman, 1990). Some scholars question the validity of the rationality hypothesis. Simon contends that individuals don't always act rationally given their limited information processing capacity, incomplete knowledge, and fluctuating preferences.

In the realm of crowdfunding, particularly campaigns explicitly directed at sustainability and circular economy, the rational choice theory has been instrumental. For instance, Hörisch (2018) employed it to understand backers' decisions to support environmentally sustainable product projects. The findings suggest that backers are motivated not just by financial gains but also by social and environmental reasons. Generally, such studies enhance the understanding of backers' motivations, providing insights for campaign organizers.

Signaling Theory and Message Framing Theory

Both the signaling theory and message framing theory are pivotal in studying persuasive communication. The signaling theory focuses on mechanisms that can mitigate informational asymmetry between parties (Spence, 1973). Specifically, it delves into how an informed party communicates (signals) and how a recipient interprets that signal (Rao et al., 2018).

Communication may involve high-cost signals, rooted in tangible actions or observable product qualities, or low-cost signals, primarily conveyed through words or images (Cheung et al., 2014). Traditionally, signals that come at a higher cost are deemed superior in addressing issues of information asymmetry compared to their low-cost counterparts (Connelly et al., 2011). For instance, gauging the caliber of an online product via a modest signal can prove arduous (Boateng, 2019). However, low-cost signals transmitted through specific framing can be invaluable when high-cost signals are hard to discern (Danilov & Sliwka, 2016).

Message framing typically oscillates between positive and negative frames. The former communicates a positive consequence (gain) if a target audience performs a specific action, while the latter highlights a negative consequence (loss) if they don't. The literature intimates that consumers are profoundly influenced by messages cast in a positive light (Maheswaran & Meyers-Levy, 1990). For favorable responses, users should adopt positive language radiating trust, credibility, reliability, and optimism. Here, the signaling theory integrates with the message framing theory, where the framing acts as a signal influencing the recipient's actions and decisions (Schamp et al., 2023).

In crowdfunding research, the signaling theory has been invoked to examine the role of project information in potential backers' decisions. Signals provided by the project are crucial for assessing its quality, and their content can influence a potential backer's funding decision. Hence, successful crowdfunding campaigns typically offer comprehensive and transparent project information to bolster backer trust and enhance project success chances (Ahlers et al., 2015). The message framing theory, meanwhile, scrutinizes how project information is presented to potential backers. How information is framed can shape perceptions of project quality and its significance to the audience. Successful crowdfunding campaigns often employ strategic framing to evoke positive emotions and convey urgency and importance.

Especially in crowdfunding campaigns explicitly geared toward environmental sustainability and circular economy, these theories analyze whether highlighting the projects' positive environmental and societal impact influences campaign success. A study by Rossolini et al. (2021) showed that crowdfunding campaigns for sustainable projects, which emphasized the social or environmental facet, fared better than those merely focusing on product presentation.

Theory of Information Diagnostics
The theory of information diagnostics centers on the degree to which information is utilized in the decision-making process (Feldman & Lynch, 1988). According to this theory, information that diminishes uncertainty during decision-making and aids consumers in their choices is seen as more diagnostic than others (Filieri, 2015). In essence, this theory examines whether the volume of information presented by a seller affects a product's perception and its subsequent likelihood of being sold. For example, Filieri (2015) delved into the impact of information on consumer choices within e-commerce settings, determining that meticulously detailed data augments purchase inclinations. In this context, the theory posits that as a webpage furnishes more elucidation to aid consumers in surmounting challenges and preconceptions born from an absence of tangible product evaluation, the information is deemed more diagnostic in guiding a discerning appraisal of the product's inherent value.

This theoretical lens is frequently harnessed in crowdfunding studies. Within crowdfunding environments, project originators often provide an encompassing narrative of the product and the journey of its genesis. Consequently, prospective backers possess enhanced tools to appraise the project and fortify their investment choices. Prior studies on overarching success determinants in crowdfunding concur that the more expansive and meticulous the project exposition, the greater its likelihood of flourishing. One such study applying the theory of information diagnostics to sustainable crowdfunding campaigns was conducted by Corsini and Frey in 2023. In their research, they assessed how the amount and quality of sustainability information affected the success rates of crowdfunding campaigns. They emphasized that campaigns providing detailed and credible sustainability practices had a higher likelihood of success than those that did not. Furthermore, campaigns that clearly and transparently communicated their sustainability practices saw increased investor engagement.

Proximity Principles
Though not strictly a theory, some crowdfunding studies lean on the concept and principles of proximity to determine its influence on campaign success.

In economic geography, the notion of proximity pertains to nearness and encompasses both geographical and non-geographical dimensions (Boschma, 2005). Boschma (2005) categorizes proximity's diverse dimensions into geographical, institutional, cognitive, social, and organizational domains. Geographical proximity, the most commonly understood facet, concerns the physical or spatial distance between economic actors. However, this is not always constant, as individuals' mobility allows for sporadic face-to-face interactions (Torre & Wallet, 2014).

Non-geographical dimensions of proximity are anchored in notions of similarity or affiliation, entailing shared knowledge, norms, values, and ties to groups, social constructs, or entities. Specifically, institutional proximity is rooted in the encompassing framework of institutions, incorporating both codified institutions like laws and guidelines, and the tacit ones, such as cultural mores, customs, and values that facilitate economic orchestration among participants (Boschma, 2005). Cognitive proximity denotes shared expertise and competencies that enhance mutual comprehension and dialogue, while social proximity focuses on trust-infused interpersonal bonds. Conversely, organizational proximity measures the degree to which relationships operate within or span across organizations, potentially curtailing ambiguities and self-interest through stringent regulatory structures (Boschma, 2005).

Proximity holds multifaceted implications, particularly in regional evolution, collaborative ventures between organizations and studies centered on the dissemination of knowledge and innovation (Knoben & Oerlemans, 2006). For example, the territorial adjacency of enterprises within a specific area can amplify direct interactions, facilitating the exchange of implicit wisdom, a phenomenon well-documented in the discourses on industrial agglomerations (Porter, 1998). Additionally, proximity analysis can pinpoint barriers to cooperation and innovation between organizations, as collaboration may be challenging with entities too distant in terms of institutional, cognitive, or organizational proximity (Bathelt et al., 2004).

The notion of geographical proximity has been invoked in some research endeavors to scrutinize the efficacy of environmental crowdfunding initiatives. For instance, an illuminating investigation by Behrendt et al. (2022) discerned that crowdfunding endeavors championing environmentally sustainable ventures in their immediate vicinity enjoyed a heightened likelihood of triumph compared to those endorsing projects located afar. This can be attributed to geographical proximity heightening the sense of community between backers and sustainable projects, thus forging a bond of trust and reciprocity (Weinmann & Mishra, 2019). Not just geographical proximity, but also cognitive proximity can play a role in crowdfunding success rates. Behrendt et al. (2022) further suggested that cognitive proximity could impact participation in crowdfunding campaigns, where backers of a particular cause might feel a kinship with campaign promoters due to shared interests or values.

5.4 Analysis of Variables Pertaining to the Crowdfunding Campaign

Based on the research outlined in Table 5.2, it is possible to delve into the primary variables influencing the success of crowdfunding campaigns explicitly geared toward sustainability and the circular economy. The subsequent sections provide a comprehensive overview of these variables as explored in academic literature.

Variables Associated with the Crowdfunding Campaign as Success Factors

Among the most extensively examined variables in academic research are those related to the actual crowdfunding campaign, such as its duration, the amount requested, and the number of campaign updates. Multiple studies have analyzed these factors (e.g., Berns et al., 2022; Corsini & Frey, 2023; Hörisch, 2018).

Empirical evidence recurrently identifies four distinct factors: the sum solicited, the diversity of rewards or revenue channels presented, the frequency of updates, and the crowdfunding category (be it reward, donation, or equity). Notably, most scholarly investigations imply that a surge in the amount sought from backers often diminishes the prospects of a crowdfunding endeavor's triumph. Various explanations could be offered for this outcome; generally, when a high amount is requested, the project becomes less accessible to a broader audience and may appear less appealing to potential financiers. Moreover, if the project demands a significant sum, a larger number of financiers is needed to meet the goal, making it more challenging to engage a sufficient number of participants. Another reason could be related to credibility: an excessively high funding request might be perceived as unrealistic and less believable. In this scenario, potential financiers might be deterred by the impression that the project is unlikely to achieve its goal.

There's also a broad agreement in the literature regarding the updates provided during a crowdfunding campaign; an increase in these often enhances the campaign's probability of success. Numerous reasons support this observation. Regular updates during a crowdfunding campaign help keep financiers engaged and interested in the project. This involvement might increase the chances of them promoting it within their network. Additionally, consistent updates can enhance the project's transparency and build trust among the financiers. Financiers are more likely to contribute if they believe the project is transparent and its progress is clearly communicated.

The number of rewards or diverse income streams offered also seems to be a pivotal factor positively affecting a sustainability-oriented crowdfunding campaign. Providing various reward options or income streams can enhance the appeal of the campaign for a wider range of financiers, accommodating different consumption preferences and businesses or investors seeking sustainable project investment opportunities with varying returns and timelines.

The last variable in this category is the type of crowdfunding. The existing literature suggests that this doesn't have a significant impact on the success probability.

A synopsis of the variables associated with the crowdfunding campaign and their influence on the triumph of environmental crowdfunding initiatives is delineated in Table 5.3.

Table 5.3 Variables pertaining to the crowdfunding campaign

Variables	Number of researches	Positive impact	Negative impact	Non-significant impact
Short duration of the campaign	4	1	1	2
Amount requested	9		7	2
High minimum investment required to become a shareholder	1		1	
Number of different rewards or income streams offered	2	2		
Number of updates	5	5		
Type of crowdfunding (reward, donation, participation)	2			2

Source Authors' elaboration

Variables Associated with Financiers as Success Factors

Among the variables identified in academic research as key success factors for crowdfunding campaigns specifically targeting sustainability and the circular economy, those related to financiers are paramount (e.g., Prędkiewicz et al., 2021; Rossolini et al., 2021). As illustrated in Table 5.4, research on this topic is in its nascent stages, with only a few studies available and substantial variances in the findings. For instance, geographic proximity has been highlighted as a variable positively influencing a crowdfunding campaign's success by Behrendt et al. (2022). In contrast, Otte and Maehle (2022) found no statistical relevance in their study between proximity and the likelihood of success.

Variables Related to Communication in Crowdfunding Campaigns

Academic inquiries have delved into the communication instruments tied to crowdfunding campaigns, deeming them pivotal for success. This

106   F. CORSINI AND M. FREY

Table 5.4 Variables associated with financiers

Variables	Number of researches	Positive impact	Negative impact	Non-significant impact
Average contribution from lenders	1			1
Number of funders	1	1		
Comments from funders	1	1		
Geographical proximity of funders to the campaign	2	1		1

Source Authors' elaboration

encompasses the magnitude of the campaign's social media following and the inclusion of a link to an external portal. Pertaining to the former, a slew of research accentuates its beneficial link with success probability (e.g., Caputo et al., 2022; Kubo et al., 2021). Within this framework, a robust social media presence can magnify a campaign's exposure, subsequently heightening its allure. Such prominence can catalyze awareness, culminating in an influx of backers. The volume of social media followers can also be tied to a credibility factor. Potential financiers might be more inclined to trust a sustainability project if they observe others endorsing it, which can heighten the likelihood of individuals supporting the initiative. The latter variable has so far been examined in one study, which indicates a positive relationship with the odds of success (Kubo et al., 2021).

A synopsis of the variables associated with communication and their influence on the triumph of environmental crowdfunding initiatives is delineated in Table 5.5.

Variables Related to the Sustainability and/or Circularity Dimensions of the Project

Most research on crowdfunding campaigns explicitly focused on sustainability and the circular economy delves into potential success variables tied to the sustainability and/or circularity dimensions of the project (e.g., Bento et al., 2019; Zhang et al., 2022). Here, the variables range from

Table 5.5 Variables related to communication

Variables	Number of researches	Positive impact	Negative impact	Non-significant impact
Number of associated social media followers	4	3		1
Presence of link to a website outside the campaign	1			1

Source Authors' elaboration

third-party endorsements about the project's sustainability to the eco-design features of the products and even the specificity of words used in the content, especially in relation to sustainability/circularity aspects (i.e., whether generic terms like "sustainable" or "ecological" are used or words that precisely outline the sustainability/circularity characteristics of the project, such as references to recycled material usage). All the variables mentioned, shown in Table 5.6, appear to be specific to individual research. They have neither been corroborated nor refuted by other studies, making it challenging to draw comprehensive insights about their potential impact on the success of such initiatives.

Variables Pertaining to the Proponent or the Proposing Team

Among the variables explored in academic research, there are those related to the proponent, the proposing team, and their description. Examples of these variables might include the percentage of women on the project's proposing team, the team's education level, or even the presence of photographs depicting team members. Within this framework, a majority of research posits that past involvement in diverse crowdfunding endeavors scarcely sways the odds of a campaign's success (Berns et al., 2022; Kubo et al., 2021). Such prior crowdfunding experience may not be a significant factor impacting the campaign's success for several reasons. For instance, having experience in an industry where funding is primarily obtained from institutional investors may not be beneficial when presenting another crowdfunding campaign in a sector where most of the funding should come from individuals. Another consideration might

108   F. CORSINI AND M. FREY

Table 5.6 Variables pertaining to the sustainability and/or circularity dimensions of the project

Variables	Number of researches	Positive impact	Negative impact	Non-significant impact
Donating a portion of the profits to charities	1	1		
Endorsement on the sustainability of the project by third parties	1	1		
Degree of positive impact of key activities on the environment and/or society	1	1		
Ecodesign features of products	1	1		
Sense of environmental urgency in the project description	1		1	
Emphasis on environmental sustainability in the title of the project	1			1
Emphasis on environmental sustainability in the body of the project description	1			1
Specificity of the words used in the text with particular reference to circularity/sustainability characteristics	1	1		

Source Authors' elaboration

be the changing market conditions; crowdfunding market conditions can vary considerably over time. For example, a proponent of a previously successful crowdfunding campaign may not be able to replicate the same success during a time when the market is more competitive or when competition has intensified. Similar insights can be drawn regarding the campaign proponent's country (Rossolini et al., 2021) and the size of the project's proposing team (Prędkiewicz et al., 2021). In both cases, available literature suggests that neither is directly linked to the success of a campaign explicitly oriented toward sustainability/circular economy.

A synopsis of the variables associated with the proponent/s and their influence on the triumph of environmental crowdfunding initiatives is delineated in Table 5.7.

Table 5.7 Variables related to the proponent, the proposing team, and their description

Variables	Number of researches	Positive impact	Negative impact	Non-significant impact
Country of the campaign promoter	2			2
Percentage of women in the project proposal team	1	1		
Size of the team proposing the project	2			2
Previous experience	5	1		4
Promoter gender	1			1
Team description	1	1		
Percentage of people graduating in the team	1	1		
Education level mentioned in the team description	1			1
Photographs of team members	1			1

Source Authors' elaboration

Variables Related to the Description and Presentation of the Project

Scientific inquiries delve deeper into variables concerning the portrayal and elucidation of the project. Such variables encompass the integration of videos or visuals in the description, the lucidity of the project's narrative, and the meticulous enumeration of milestones.

As delineated in the subsequent table, prevailing research indicates that for endeavors distinctly aligned with sustainability or the circular economy, the infusion of videos or imagery within the project narrative bears little influence on its success prospects (Kubo et al., 2021). In this milieu, crowdfunding pursuits promoting sustainable initiatives might captivate patrons already attuned to the significance of sustainability. Hence, they remain largely indifferent to the embellishment of the narrative with videos or visuals. Here, the quality of the project description might be a more significant factor than the presence of videos or images. A detailed and accurate project description, which clearly and persuasively explains the objectives, benefits, and environmental impact, could be more effective in convincing backers to support the project, even without videos or images. Indeed, each of the trio of studies at hand suggests that the word count employed to elucidate the project favorably steers the success trajectory of the crowdfunding campaign (Corsini & Frey, 2021).

A synopsis of the variables related to the description and presentation of the project and their influence on the success of environmental crowdfunding initiatives is delineated in Table 5.8.

Variables Pertaining to the Reference Market

Among the variables explored in academic research, there are also those related to the project's target market. The two variables under investigation, as shown in the table below, are the number of potential competitors for the project and the type of market the project targets (niche market or mass market). In this context, both Hörisch (2018) and Corsini and Frey (2023) emphasize that projects aimed at niche markets have a higher probability of success compared to those intended for mass markets. Potential reasons for this finding could be rooted in the more focused approach to the specific needs of niche markets; projects tailored for niche markets might be designed and developed more precisely to meet the unique demands of their reference market. Such projects might hold more relevance and appeal to potential backers, thereby increasing the likelihood of crowdfunding success. Another rationale could be the reduced competition. In a niche market, competition among projects might be less intense compared to a mass market, granting projects increased visibility and a better chance of success. Furthermore, environmental or circular economy-related projects targeting niche markets could be perceived as innovative and distinct compared to the more generic projects aimed at mass markets. This uniqueness could captivate backers and boost the success chances of these campaigns.

A synopsis of the variables related to the reference market and their influence on the success of environmental crowdfunding initiatives is delineated in Table 5.9.

5 SUCCESS FACTORS IN SUSTAINABILITY ... 111

Table 5.8 Variables related to the description and presentation of the project

Variables	Number of researches	Positive impact	Negative impact	Non-significant impact
Campaign objectives presented with quantitative data	1	1		
Presence of figures in the project description	3		1	2
Presence of videos in the project description	6	1	1	4
Number of words used to describe the project	3	3		
Number of tags used to present the project	1	1		
Precise description of key project milestones	1			1
Readability of the text related to the project description	1			1

Source Authors' elaboration

Table 5.9 Variables related to the reference market

Variables	Number of searches	Positive impact	Negative impact	Non-significant impact
Number of potential competitors of the project	1		1	
Type of market to which the project is addressed	2	2		

Source Authors' elaboration

112   F. CORSINI AND M. FREY

Table 5.10   Variables related to the perceived quality and progress of the project

Variables	Number of searches	Positive impact	Negative impact	Non-significant impact
Technical quality of the project	1			1
Innovativeness of the product/ project	2	1		1
Project aimed at satisfying a need never satisfied before for the user	1			1
Project progress	1			1

Source Authors' elaboration

Variables Related to the Perceived Quality and Progress of the Project

The concluding set of variables dissected in scholarly explorations of success determinants for crowdfunding endeavors, especially those aligned with sustainability and the circular economy, relates to the project's perceived caliber and ongoing advancement. The said variables are showcased in Table 5.10. Their presence seems intrinsic to specific research, with no supporting or opposing evidence in other academic works. Hence, drawing extensive conclusions about their bearing on the triumph of such ventures remains intricate.

5.5   CONCLUSIONS

The chapter endeavors to encapsulate studies traversing two veins of literature; firstly, those aspiring to ascertain whether environmental sustainability intrinsically is a trait conducive to crowdfunding triumph, and secondly, those exclusively delving into projects with environmental hallmarks, striving to discern the attributes propelling the success of these singular initiatives.

The scrutiny of the initial segment of research seemingly insinuates that environmental sustainability, in certain specific cases, might epitomize a success factor in crowdfunding.

Upon examining studies that focus exclusively on projects with environmental characteristics to identify the factors contributing to the success of these unique endeavors, a wide range of variables associated with the success of such initiatives was identified and described. However, research on the success of environmental or circular crowdfunding is still in its early stages, indicating the need for further investigation. This chapter, therefore, serves as a foundation for understanding what has been explored in this domain and outlines potential directions for future research.

References

Ahlers, G. K., Cumming, D., Günther, C., & Schweizer, D. (2015). Signaling in equity crowdfunding. *Entrepreneurship Theory and Practice, 39*(4), 955–980.

Barasinska, N., & Schäfer, D. (2014). Is crowdfunding different? Evidence on the relation between gender and funding success from a German peer-to-peer lending platform. *German Economic Review, 15*(4), 436–452.

Bathelt, H., Malmberg, A., & Maskell, P. (2004). Clusters and knowledge: Local buzz, global pipelines, and the process of knowledge creation. *Progress in Human Geography, 28*(1), 31–56.

Becker, G. (1976). *The economic approach to human behavior.* University of Chicago Press.

Belleflamme, P., Lambert, T., & Schwienbacher, A. (2014). Crowdfunding: Tapping the right crowd. *Journal of Business Venturing, 29*(5), 585–609.

Behrendt, G., Peter, S., Sterly, S., & Häring, A. M. (2022). Community financing for sustainable food and farming: A proximity perspective. *Agriculture and Human Values, 39*(3), 1063–1075.

Bento, N., Gianfrate, G., & Thoni, M. H. (2019). Crowdfunding for sustainability ventures. *Journal of Cleaner Production, 237*, 117751.

Bernardino, S., & Santos, J. F. (2021). Assessing risk in lending crowdfunding: An investor and platform manager perspective. *International Journal of Entrepreneurial Venturing, 13*(4), 382–403.

Berns, J. P., Jia, Y., & Gondo, M. (2022). Crowdfunding success in sustainability-oriented projects: An exploratory examination of the crowdfunding of 3D printers. *Technology in Society, 71*, 102099.

Boateng, S. L. (2019). Online relationship marketing and customer loyalty: A signaling theory perspective. *International Journal of Bank Marketing, 37*(1), 226–240.

Boschma, R. (2005). Proximity and innovation: A critical assessment. *Regional Studies, 39*(1), 61–74.

Bukhari, F. A. S., Usman, S. M., Usman, M., & Hussain, K. (2020). The effects of creator credibility and backer endorsement in donation crowdfunding campaigns success. *Baltic Journal of Management, 15*(2), 215–235.

Calic, G., & Mosakowski, E. (2016). Kicking off social entrepreneurship: How a sustainability orientation influences crowdfunding success. *Journal of Management Studies, 53*(5), 738–767.

Cappa, F., Pinelli, M., Maiolini, R., & Leone, M. I. (2021). "Pledge" me your ears! The role of narratives and narrator experience in explaining crowdfunding success. *Small Business Economics, 57*(2), 953–973.

Caputo, A., Schiocchet, E., & Troise, C. (2022). Sustainable business models as successful drivers in equity crowdfunding. *Business Strategy and the Environment, 31*(7), 3509–3522.

Chakraborty, S., & Swinney, R. (2021). Signaling to the crowd: Private quality information and rewards-based crowdfunding. *Manufacturing & Service Operations Management, 23*(1), 155–169.

Chamberlin, E. H. (1974). *The theory of Monopolistic competition: A Re-orientation of the theory of value*. Harvard University Press.

Chan, C. R., Park, H. D., Patel, P., & Gomulya, D. (2018). Reward-based crowdfunding success: Decomposition of the project, product category, entrepreneur, and location effects. *Venture Capital, 20*(3), 285–307.

Chan, H. F., Moy, N., Schaffner, M., & Torgler, B. (2021). The effects of money saliency and sustainability orientation on reward-based crowdfunding success. *Journal of Business Research, 125*, 443–455.

Chen, Y., Dai, R., Wang, L., Yang, S., Li, Y., & Wei, J. (2021). Exploring donor's intention in charitable crowdfunding: Intrinsic and extrinsic motivations. *Industrial Management & Data Systems, 121*(7), 1664–1683.

Cheung, C. M., Lee, M. K., & Rabjohn, N. (2014). The impact of electronic word-of-mouth: The adoption of online opinions in online customer communities. *Internet Research, 24*(5), 597–624.

Clauss, T., Niemand, T., Kraus, S., Schnetzer, P., & Brem, A. (2020). Increasing crowdfunding success through social media: The importance of reach and utilization in reward-based crowdfunding. *International Journal of Innovation Management, 24*(03), 2050026.

Coakley, J., Lazos, A., & Liñares-Zegarra, J. M. (2022). Equity crowdfunding founder teams: Campaign success and venture failure. *British Journal of Management, 33*(1), 286–305.

Coleman, J. S. (1990). *Foundations of social theory*. Harvard University Press.

Connelly, B. L., Certo, S. T., Ireland, R. D., & Reutzel, C. R. (2011). Signaling theory: A review and assessment. *Journal of Management, 37*(1), 39–67.

Corsini, F., & Frey, M. (2021). Exploring the development of environmentally sustainable products through reward-based crowdfunding. *Electronic Commerce Research, 23*(1), 1–25.

Corsini, F., & Frey, M. (2023). Crowdfunding sustainable products with the product search matrix: Niche markets vs. mass markets. *Electronic Commerce Research*, 1–26.

Dalla Chiesa, C., Pavlova, A., Lavanga, M., & Pysana, N. (2022). When fashion meets crowdfunding: Exploring sustainable and innovative features of online campaigns. *Journal of Fashion Marketing and Management*, Vol. ahead-of-print No. ahead-of-print. https://doi.org/10.1108/JFMM-03-2021-0068.

Danilov, A., & Sliwka, D. (2017). Can contracts signal social norms? *Experimental Evidence. Management Science, 63*(2), 459–476.

De Crescenzo, V., Ribeiro-Soriano, D. E., & Covin, J. G. (2020). Exploring the viability of equity crowdfunding as a fundraising instrument: A configurational analysis of contingency factors that lead to crowdfunding success and failure. *Journal of Business Research, 115*, 348–356.

Deci, E. L. (1971). Effects of externally mediated rewards on intrinsic motivation. *Journal of Personality and Social Psychology, 18*(1), 105–115.

Deci, E. L., & Ryan, R. M. (1980). The empirical exploration of intrinsic motivational processes. *Advances in Experimental Social Psychology, 13*, 39–80.

Deci, E. L., & Ryan, R. M. (2008). Self-determination theory: A macrotheory of human motivation, development, and health. *Canadian Psychology/Psychologie Canadienne, 49*(3), 182–185.

Drover, W., Busenitz, L., Matusik, S., Townsend, D., Anglin, A., & Dushnitsky, G. (2017). A review and road map of entrepreneurial equity financing research: Venture capital, corporate venture capital, angel investment, crowdfunding, and accelerators. *Journal of Management, 43*(6), 1820–1853.

Feldman, J. M., & Lynch, J. G. (1988). Self-generated validity and other effects of measurement on belief, attitude, intention, and behavior. *Journal of Applied Psychology, 73*(3), 421–435.

Filieri, R. (2015). What makes online reviews helpful? A diagnosticity adoption framework to explain informational and normative influences in e-WOM. *Journal of Business Research, 68*(6), 1261–1270.

Freeman, R. E. (1984). *Strategic management: A stakeholder approach.* Cambridge University Press.

Gorbatai, A., & Nelson, L. (2015). The narrative advantage: Gender and the language of crowdfunding. *Haas School of Business UC Berkeley. Research Papers*, 1–32.

Hansmann, H. (1980). The role of nonprofit enterprise. *The Yale Law Journal, 89*(5), 835–901.

Hansmann, H. B. (1987). Economic theories of nonprofit organizations. In *the nonprofit sector: A research handbook* (pp. 27–42). Yale University Press.

Hardin, G. (1982). Collective action as an agreeable n-prisoner's dilemma. *Behavioral Science, 27*(1), 21–36.

Hörisch, J. (2015). Crowdfunding for environmental ventures: An empirical analysis of the influence of environmental orientation on the success of crowdfunding initiatives. *Journal of Cleaner Production, 107*, 636–645.

Hörisch, J. (2018). Think big' or 'small is beautiful'? An empirical analysis of characteristics and determinants of success of sustainable crowdfunding projects. *International Journal of Entrepreneurial Venturing, 10*(1), 111–129.

Hörisch, J., & Tenner, I. (2020). How environmental and social orientations influence the funding success of investment-based crowdfunding: The mediating role of the number of funders and the average funding amount. *Technological Forecasting and Social Change, 161*, 120311.

Hornuf, L., & Neuenkirch, M. (2017). Pricing shares in equity crowdfunding. *Small Business Economics, 48*, 795–811.

Kahneman, D., & Tversky, A. (1979). Prospect theory: An analysis of decision under risk. *Econometrica, 47*(2), 263–291.

Kgoroeadira, R., Burke, A., & van Stel, A. (2019). Small business online loan crowdfunding: Who gets funded and what determines the rate of interest? *Small Business Economics, 52*, 67–87.

Knoben, J., & Oerlemans, L. A. G. (2006). Proximity and inter-organizational collaboration: A literature review. *International Journal of Management Reviews, 8*(2), 71–89.

Kubo, T., Veríssimo, D., Uryu, S., Mieno, T., & MacMillan, D. (2021). What determines the success and failure of environmental crowdfunding? *Ambio, 50*, 1659–1669.

Kunz, M. M., Bretschneider, U., Erler, M., & Leimeister, J. M. (2018). An empirical investigation of signaling in reward-based crowdfunding. *Electronic Commerce Research, 17*, 425–461.

Lagazio, C., & Querci, F. (2018). Exploring the multi-sided nature of crowdfunding campaign success. *Journal of Business Research, 90*, 318–324.

Li, Y., Liu, F., Fan, W., Lim, E. T., & Liu, Y. (2022). Exploring the impact of initial herd on overfunding in equity crowdfunding. *Information & Management, 59*(3), 103269.

Ljumović, I., Pavlović, V., & Knežević, G. (2021). Financing agri-food business in the Mediterranean area through crowdfunding: Do environmental issues matter? *New Medit, 3*, 101–117.

Lukk, M., Schneiderhan, E., & Soares, J. (2018). Worthy? Crowdfunding the Canadian health care and education sectors. *Canadian Review of Sociology/ revue Canadienne De Sociologie, 55*(3), 404–424.

Maheswaran, D., & Meyers-Levy, J. (1990). The influence of message framing and issue involvement. *Journal of Marketing Research, 27*(3), 361–367.

Marwell, G., & Oliver, P. (1993). *The critical mass in collective action: A micro-social theory*. Cambridge University Press.

Mastrangelo, L., Cruz-Ros, S., & Miquel-Romero, M. J. (2020). Crowdfunding success: The role of co-creation, feedback, and corporate social responsibility. *International Journal of Entrepreneurial Behavior & Research, 26*(3), 449–466.

Motylska-Kuzma, A. (2018). Crowdfunding and sustainable development. *Sustainability, 10*(12), 4650.

Olson, M. (1965). *The Logic of collective action: Public goods and the theory of groups.* Harvard University Press.

Otte, P. P., & Maehle, N. (2022). The combined effect of success factors in crowdfunding of cleantech projects. *Journal of Cleaner Production, 366,* 132921.

Porter, M. E. (1998). Clusters and the new economics of competition. *Harvard Business Review, 76*(6), 77–90.

Prędkiewicz, K., & Kalinowska-Beszczyńska, O. (2021). Financing eco-projects: Analysis of factors influencing the success of crowdfunding campaigns. *International Journal of Entrepreneurial Behavior & Research, 27*(2), 547–566.

Ralcheva, A., & Roosenboom, P. (2020). Forecasting success in equity crowdfunding. *Small Business Economics, 55,* 39–56.

Rao, S., Lee, K. B., Connelly, B., & Iyengar, D. (2018). Return time leniency in online retail: A signaling theory perspective on buying outcomes. *Decision Sciences, 49*(2), 275–305.

Reinboth, M., & Duda, J. L. (2006). Perceived motivational climate, need satisfaction and indices of well-being in team sports: A longitudinal perspective. *Psychology of Sport and Exercise, 7*(3), 269–286.

Rossolini, M., Pedrazzoli, A., & Ronconi, A. (2021). Greening crowdfunding campaigns: An investigation of message framing and effective communication strategies for funding success. *International Journal of Bank Marketing, 39*(7), 1395–1419.

Ryan, R. M., & Deci, E. L. (2000). Self-determination theory and the facilitation of intrinsic motivation, social development, and well-being. *American Psychologist, 55*(1), 68–78.

Schamp, C., Heitmann, M., Bijmolt, T. H., & Katzenstein, R. (2023). The effectiveness of cause-related marketing: A meta-analysis on consumer responses. *Journal of Marketing Research, 60*(1), 189–215.

Scott, W. R. (1987). The adolescence of institutional theory. *Administrative Science Quarterly,* 493–511.

Sheldon, K. M., & Niemiec, C. P. (2006). It's not just the amount that counts: Balanced need satisfaction also affects well-being. *Journal of Personality and Social Psychology, 91*(2), 331–341.

Smith, A. (1776). An inquiry into the nature and causes of the wealth of nations: Volume One. London: printed for W. Strahan; and T. Cadell.

Shneor, R., & Vik, A. A. (2020). Crowdfunding success: A systematic literature review 2010–2017. *Baltic Journal of Management, 15*(2), 149–182.

Siebeneicher, S., & Bock, C. (2022). Sustainable aim and personal gain? How sustainable value affects the relation between personal value and crowdfunding success. *Technological Forecasting and Social Change, 183,* 121938.

Siebeneicher, S., Yenice, I., & Bock, C. (2022). Financial-return crowdfunding for energy and sustainability in the German-speaking realm. *Sustainability, 14*(19), 12239.

Spence, M. (1973). Job market signaling. *The Quarterly Journal of Economics, 87*(3), 355–374.

Suchman, M. C. (1995). Managing legitimacy: Strategic and institutional approaches. *Academy of management review, 20*(3), 571–610.

Torre, A., & Wallet, F. (Eds.). (2014). *Regional development and proximity relations*. Edward Elgar Publishing.

Varian, H. R. (1992). *Microeconomic analysis*. W. W. Norton & Company.

Vismara, S. (2019). Sustainability in equity crowdfunding. *Technological Forecasting and Social Change, 141*, 98–106.

Wang, Z., & Yang, X. (2019). Understanding backers' funding intention in reward crowdfunding: An elaboration likelihood perspective. *Technology in Society, 58*, 101149.

Weinmann, M., & Mishra, A. (2019). *The effect of social distance in donation-based crowdfunding*. SSRN 3524087.

Witztum, A. (2005). Social circumstances and rationality: Some lessons from Adam Smith why we may not all be equally sovereign. *American Journal of Economics and Sociology, 64*(4), 1025–1047.

Yuan, H., Lau, R. Y., & Xu, W. (2016). The determinants of crowdfunding success: A semantic text analytics approach. *Decision Support Systems, 91*, 67–76.

Zhang, W., Yan, X., & Chen, Y. (2017). Configurational path to financing performance of crowdfunding projects using fuzzy set qualitative comparative analysis. *Engineering Economics, 28*(1), 25–34.

Zhang, Y., Tan, C. D., Sun, J., & Yang, Z. (2020). Why do people patronize donation-based crowdfunding platforms? An activity perspective of critical success factors. *Computers in Human Behavior, 112*, 106470.

Zhang, X. Y., Tu, J. C., Gu, S., Lu, T. H., & Yi, M. (2022). Construct and priority ranking of factors affecting crowdfunding for green products. *Processes, 10*(3), 480.

Ziegler, T., & Shneor, R. (2020). Lending crowdfunding: principles and market development. *Advances in crowdfunding:* Research and practice, 63–92.

CHAPTER 6

Crowdfunding, Fraudfunding, and Greenwashing

Abstract The crowdfunding market remains an instrument in its developmental phase, yet it's witnessing swift growth. Like all novel tools, crowdfunding must prove its capability to fulfill unmet needs within the current market. To establish credibility, it is crucial to curb deceptive practices that undermine the reputation of the tool. This chapter begins with a review of the types of fraud in crowdfunding and then frames greenwashing as a potential category of fraud based on environmental claims within crowdfunding. Indeed, greenwashing refers to the practice of portraying projects as environmentally friendly or sustainable, even when they are not. Such deceptive practices can be considered fraudulent, particularly as backers interested in supporting green initiatives may be misled. Building on original data acquired through a questionnaire submitted to creators of crowdfunding campaigns, this chapter also aims to investigate the perception of the greenwashing phenomenon by upcoming creators and their views on the role of platforms in mitigating the phenomenon. Finally, the conclusions of the chapter focus on several recommendations on how to discourage fraud and greenwashing in crowdfunding.

Keywords Crowdfunding fraud · Investor deception · Greenwashing · Perception · Claim verification

© The Author(s), under exclusive license to Springer Nature 119
Switzerland AG 2024
F. Corsini and M. Frey, *Crowdfunding for Environmental Sustainability and the Circular Economy*,
https://doi.org/10.1007/978-3-031-66211-9_6

6.1 Fraud in Crowdfunding: A Taxonomy of Fraudfunding

Offering a definitive description of fraud within crowdfunding is challenging, especially since to date, few cases have been legally identified as scams. Various studies have attempted to provide definitions of fraud across diverse crowdfunding types (Belavina et al., 2020; Hainz, 2018). Yet, a definition encompassing all types, as outlined by Cummings et al. (2021), posits that an individual committing fraud through a crowdfunding campaign:

1. Delivers false statements about the project or provides unclear information on its specifics;
2. Is aware of the falsehood of the claim;
3. Intends to deceive investors through these claims.

Further clarifying, Cummings et al. (2021) suggest that a defrauded investor should meet the following conditions:

4. Must have reasonably relied on the fundraiser's claims;
5. Must have been harmed due to the fundraiser's actions.

Consequently, fraud emerges when the fraudulent endeavors escape notice throughout the duration of the campaign, enabling the initiators to secure the amassed capital. Subsequently, backers might discover, for instance, that the creators deliberately misrepresented facts or that the entire project was a sham. Mollick (2014), having analyzed over 23,000 reward-based crowdfunding projects on Kickstarter from 2009 to 2012, identified that 2.9% of the sample comprised subjects who secured funding only to vanish later.

Not every attempted fraud by organizations in crowdfunding results in loss. Some frauds are prevented when platforms reject suspicious campaigns before they start, or vigilant backers spot and halt dishonest campaigns before funds are exchanged. While there is no comprehensive database of all fraud cases in crowdfunding, resources like GoFraudMe track attempted and actual frauds in donation-based campaigns, and Kickscammed allows users to report suspicious activities in reward-based crowdfunding. However, detecting every potential fraud remains difficult, particularly when some campaigns fail quietly without any financial transactions.

There exist some gray areas where it's hard to determine the presence of fraud. For instance, there have been cases where project creators, aiming to achieve the initially identified capital requirement, have directly contributed to their campaigns (Cummings et al., 2021). Many platforms operate on an "all or nothing" principle, where project promoters receive funds only if they meet the preset funding goal. Such self-funding might reside in a gray zone: it might display genuine intent to kick-start a project, but could simultaneously be perceived as fraudulent.

Lastly, recent years have witnessed the emergence of numerous niche platforms, elevating the risk of platform-based fraud. The more platforms there are, the higher the likelihood that platform operators might engage in or permit fraudulent activities. Although this remains a valid category, no cases have been reported as of yet (Cummings et al., 2021).

Frauds in Donation-Based Crowdfunding

Donation-based crowdfunding has become a popular method for raising funds for personal projects, emergencies, and charities. As its popularity grows, so does the risk of fraud. Unlike traditional fundraising that relies on familiar contacts, crowdfunding reaches a wider audience at low cost, which increases the potential for scams. Backers often lack straightforward methods to verify the legitimacy of campaigns, making it easy for fraudulent ones to solicit donations for false causes or emotional appeals. For example, some campaigns in the United States have falsely sought funds by posing as war veterans (Ho et al., 2021).

The striking resemblance between a legitimate and a fraudulent campaign makes it challenging for a potential donor to distinguish between the two. Perez et al. (2022) recently studied 700 donation-based crowdfunding campaigns, constructing a machine-learning classifier to identify potentially fraudulent campaigns. According to their results, emotions such as joy, sadness, and fear are wielded and balanced similarly in both genuine and fraudulent campaigns.

Due to these nuances, platforms are increasingly taking the responsibility of screening for fraudulent activities. In charitable campaigns, the end beneficiary is often aware of the campaign. However, there are instances when campaigns are initiated without the beneficiary's knowledge. To prevent scams, many platforms have established processes allowing a purported beneficiary, upon discovering a campaign initiated in their name, to either formally be named the beneficiary or to report the campaign if they suspect it's fraudulent.

Perceived Frauds and Performance Issues in Reward-Based Crowdfunding

The previous section primarily addressed actual fraudulent activities. However, in some situations, we are dealing with what might be termed "perceived frauds" or more aptly, performance issues, particularly evident in reward-based crowdfunding.

In this model, allegations of fraud frequently arise when there are significant delays in delivering rewards. In reward-based crowdfunding, backers essentially pre-order an anticipated version of the new product they are supporting in exchange for their contribution. Within this framework, aspiring businesses can face delays, and it is not uncommon for backers to wait substantially longer than initially promised during the campaign. In some extreme cases, the funded entity may even fail, leaving backers without their promised product.

In cases of mere delay, it is more appropriate to term these as performance issues rather than frauds unless there's a deliberate intent by the company to deceive investors. However, distinguishing between genuinely fraudulent projects and those that faced unexpected setbacks or failed can be challenging.

Mollick's, 2014 research noted that out of 471 design and technology projects with deadlines before July 2012, 14 projects failed, with only three reimbursing their backers. Moreover, 126 projects (approximately 33%) experienced an average delay of about 2.4 months in delivering rewards, highlighting the performance issues inherent in this crowdfunding model. These delays can arise from financial mismanagement, technical problems, or even fraudulent intentions.

Another significant performance issue arises when rewards undergo significant alterations compared to what was promised during the crowdfunding campaign. This discrepancy could stem from technical issues, funding management challenges, or genuine fraudulent intent by the company.

Within the framework of the circular economy, the Solar Roadways initiative offers a pertinent example (Solar Roadways, 2014). This crowd-funding endeavor, which gained widespread attention in 2014, advocated for the incorporation of solar panels into roadways as a means of electricity generation. Additionally, these panels were designed to light up roads via LED technology and to melt accumulated snow or ice through embedded heating coils.

Initiated on the Indiegogo platform, the campaign swiftly garnered over $2.2 million. However, the promises seemed too good to be true. Skepticism arose, both due to the exorbitant production costs and the speculated subpar performance of the embedded solar panels. The pilot installation in Sandpoint, Idaho, in 2016 covered roughly 14 square meters with 30 panels costing around $60,000. These panels generated an average daily energy of approximately 0.25 kWh during peak solar months—much less than a standard domestic solar panel. A subsequent installation in Baltimore, Maryland, in 2019 performed only marginally better.

Solar Roadways exemplifies performance issues in crowdfunding, not fraud. Often, promises made during fundraising are ambitious and potentially unrealistic, leading to disappointing outcomes.

Frauds in Loan-Based Crowdfunding

Currently, there is limited data on fraud in loan-based crowdfunding. Studies like the one by Iyer et al. (2015) have attempted to use default rates on the Prosper platform as a proxy to gauge fraud. Their analysis covered over 17,000 three-year, fixed-rate loans issued between February 2007 and October 2008, revealing a default rate of 30.6% that varied significantly by credit category. For instance, in the lowest credit category, the default rate was as high as 51.6%, while in the highest, it was 14.7%.

These default rates are influenced by the economic context at the time, particularly the 2007–2008 financial crisis, which likely exacerbated the challenges faced by borrowers. Comparatively, commercial bank default rates during the same period were lower, with residential mortgages at about 10.5% in 2010 and consumer credit card loans peaking at 6.8% in 2009, as documented in Iyer et al. (2015). This context helps highlight the relative risk associated with peer-to-peer lending during economic downturns.

The information in Fig. 6.1 invites contemplation. Initially, it's clear that the 14.7% default rate for Prosper's most creditworthy borrowers surpasses the industry norm. This suggests that individuals borrowing through Prosper were less disposed to fulfill their repayment obligations compared to those seeking funds from conventional lenders. Yet, it's crucial to emphasize that borrowers in Prosper's high-risk categories are often those who would face extreme difficulty, if not outright impossibility, in obtaining loans from mainstream banking institutions. Viewed from this angle, Prosper's default rates may not be extraordinarily divergent from those observed in the traditional lending landscape. Although these figures can portray the trend of loans via crowdfunding platforms, it remains unclear whether defaults were intentional or if borrowers faced repayment challenges. This ambiguity further complicates the depiction of the phenomenon of fraud in loan-based crowdfunding.

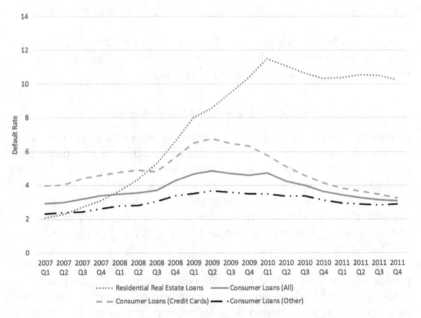

Fig. 6.1 Default rates reported by commercial banks (2023) (*Source* Authors' elaboration based on Federal Reserve data)

Frauds in Equity Crowdfunding

As outlined in Chapter 3, equity crowdfunding is a profit-sharing model between the campaign initiator and the financiers. Essentially, through equity crowdfunding, an entrepreneur invites investors to contribute funds in exchange for a share in the company's future earnings.

This form of crowdfunding is relatively recent, and thus, there's limited research on the performance of businesses financed via equity crowdfunding platforms. Presently, there seems to be an absence of studies on fraudulent behaviors within this funding model.

Signori and Vismara (2016) examined 212 equity crowdfunding campaigns funded through the British platform Crowdcube between 2011 and 2015. From this sample, the authors identified 22 (10.4%) failed projects, resulting in a -100% return for investors. Another 126 projects (59.4%) yielded a zero return; these companies neither failed nor sought additional financial ventures. Finally, the average return from investments in 64 (30.2%) companies that raised further capital in equity operations was 63.5%. When weighing the returns, the authors estimated an expected yield of 8.8% on investments in initial equity crowdfunding offerings.

Hornuf and Schmitt (2016), studying 303 campaigns on German equity crowdfunding platforms, reported findings akin to the earlier mentioned study. Notably, they highlight that 85% of the funded companies remain operational three years after receiving their funds. This survival rate surpasses the general startup population in Germany, which stands at 70%. The findings from both studies might suggest that fraud in equity crowdfunding is relatively rare. This could be attributed to the stringent selection criteria of equity crowdfunding platforms, determining which businesses gain platform access. Through this process, most applicants, including potentially fraudulent ones, are weeded out during platform entry.

While the aforementioned data doesn't allude to wrongful practices by entrepreneurs using this crowdfunding type, the rising number of platforms hosting such campaigns could increase platform-related fraud risks. A recent report (Ziegler et al., 2021) indicates that alternatives to traditional financing have been around for over a decade (Fig. 6.2). Still, some countries lack proper regulations to oversee crowdfunding operations, especially concerning equity crowdfunding (see Fig. 5.4). While North America, Europe, and China have successfully adopted a regulatory

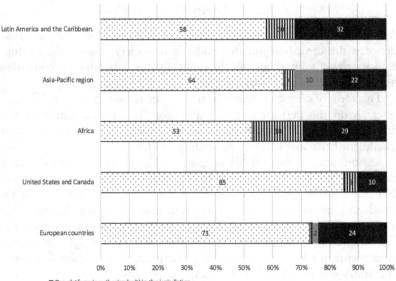

Fig. 6.2 Licensing status of equity crowdfunding platforms (*Source* Adapted from Ziegler et al., 2021)

framework for these novel fundraising activities, others lag behind (refer to Fig. 5.2). For instance, equity crowdfunding remains a loosely regulated domain in India and South Africa (Ziegler et al., 2021). Unlicensed platforms, operating fundraising activities illicitly, could pose a significant threat to novice investors, amplifying fraud risks.

6.2 Greenwashing as a Form of Fraud

The growing focus on environmental issues among consumers has brought to light the phenomenon of greenwashing. This tendency first came into focus in 1986, thanks to activist Jay Westerveld, who noted that hotels were encouraging guests to reuse towels, purporting it as an eco-friendly measure aimed at conserving water and energy. Westerveld pointed out that these hotels had many other environmental concerns to address before turning their attention to towels.

Since then, the phenomenon of greenwashing has been studied and analyzed in various contexts and sectors. There have been numerous definitions provided to describe this trend, some of which are listed in Table 6.1.

From the definitions previously discussed, it becomes clear that the objective of greenwashing tactics is to mislead consumers regarding either a company's ecological practices or the environmental advantages of a specific product or service. In both scenarios, greenwashing can be perceived as fraudulent since it involves the deceptive use of environmental information to promote businesses, products, or services, intending to convince consumers of their sustainability when, in fact, they are not. This behavior can be seen as deceitful because it seeks to gain undue competitive advantage based on false or misleading information. Moreover, consumers might base their purchasing decisions on such deceptive information, thinking they're making an eco-friendly choice when they are not. This can lead to adverse environmental consequences, making greenwashing not only an unfair practice but also potentially harmful.

Table 6.1 Definitions of greenwashing

Definition	Source
Greenwashing is "the act of misleading consumers regarding the environmental practices of a company or the environmental performance and positive communication about environmental performance."	TerraChoice (2010)
Greenwashing is represented by "poor environmental performance and positive communication about environmental performance."	Delmas and Burbano (2011)
Greenwashing is "the act of disseminating disinformation to consumers regarding the environmental practices of a company or the environmental benefits of a product or service."	Baum (2012)
Greenwashing is a "communication that misleads people regarding environmental performance/benefits by disclosing negative information and disseminating positive information about an organization, service, or product."	Tateishi (2018)

Source Authors' elaboration

Greenwashing occurs for numerous reasons. Delmas and Burbano (2011) analyzed the issue through institutional theory, emphasizing the significance of regulatory, normative, and cognitive factors in shaping company decisions on specific organizational practices. The regulatory framework is a crucial external institutional factor prompting corporate greenwashing. Greenwashing regulations in Europe and the United States are quite limited, and their enforcement is often uncertain. With this scant regulatory oversight, there are few legal repercussions for companies adopting this strategy.

Yet, institutional factors alone can't explain the variance in company strategies. Market factors are also vital drivers of greenwashing (Delmas & Burbano, 2011). This behavior is primarily driven by a company's ability to enhance its market share through differentiation. Currently, both consumers and investors are growing more predisposed to opt for sustainable products. Numerous companies enhance their standing by introducing "eco-friendly" offerings. At the same time, other research emphasizes that a significant number of consumers are prepared to pay an extra amount for products deemed sustainable (Nielsen Media Research, 2015). The combined increase in environmental awareness and consumers' readiness to alter their buying habits has escalated environmental marketing by firms and the concurrent rise in deceptive greenwashing practices. In addition, there is a substantial growth of "green investors" who specifically aim to invest in firms with commendable environmental sustainability performances. In this setting, firms are pressured both by consumers and investors to appear environmentally conscious and, thus are inclined to positively portray their environmental performance, especially since there are minimal legal or regulatory consequences for doing so.

The competitive landscape is another potential incentive for greenwashing (Delmas & Burbano, 2011). Companies often mold their behaviors based on the perceived successful practices of similar firms. In this context, some might promote sustainable practices merely for fear of lagging behind competitors who have already started doing so.

Additionally, firm characteristics play a pivotal role in moderating a company's response to external drivers and either facilitating or discouraging greenwashing activities (Gatti et al., 2019). Attributes such as a company's scale, sector, profitability, stage in its life cycle, and particular skills and assets shape its overarching strategic decisions, the associated economic pros and cons of particular courses of action, and the degree to which the firm perceives external pressures. Moreover, a firm's incentive structure and ethical climate can be indicative of its ethical behavior. Therefore, both incentives and ethical climate might propel unethical behaviors like greenwashing.

Lastly, it's crucial to note the significant role of individual company managers. Their actions are instrumental in explaining a company's behavior (Santos et al., 2023). In this respect, unethical behaviors or biases stemming from preconceived notions, personal preferences, deep-seated beliefs, or even a limited understanding of environmental topics can give rise to greenwashing within a company.

How Is Greenwashing Manifested?

Much of the available academic and non-academic literature has focused on product/service level greenwashing to highlight the most frequently used misleading textual arguments in this practice. There are several examples of how product greenwashing is carried out; TerraChoice (2010) identifies 7 sins of greenwashing (Table 6.2).

This type of greenwashing, in the context of crowdfunding, is a practice that can be implemented in campaigns aimed at creating a product and thus based on rewards. In this setting, a possible example of greenwashing could be represented by Miramir (Champagne & Gianfrate, 2020). The project aims to develop "a new alternative social ecosystem to unite those who care about our planet and the future of the human race" (Miramir, 2017). Both in the summary presentation of the product and in the project description, as well as in the introductory video, many generic terms are used, along with vague information lacking industry standards or figures to better understand the possible environmental benefits of this initiative (Champagne & Gianfrate, 2020).

Greenwashing is not a practice limited solely to the product level but also occurs at the corporate level. In this context, Contreras-Pacheco and Claasen (2017) have identified five forms of corporate greenwashing, which are presented in Table 6.3.

An example of corporate-level greenwashing could be considered General Electric's "Ecomagination" campaign, which publicized the organization's environmental practices while simultaneously lobbying against new air emissions requirements set forth by the United States Environmental Protection Agency (EPA) (Delmas & Burbano, 2011). Corporate-level greenwashing activities could be encountered in equity

130   F. CORSINI AND M. FREY

Table 6.2 Forms of product greenwashing implementation

Sins	Description	Example
Sin of the hidden trade-off	It is distinguished by an assertion that a product is eco-friendly based on select attributes, while ignoring other crucial environmental factors	For example, paper's environmental footprint is not necessarily diminished simply because it hails from responsibly managed woodlands. Other ecological factors, such as chlorine use in the bleaching process, can carry comparable significance
Sin of no proof	It is marked by an eco-conscious assertion not substantiated by easily available information or independent verification	Frequent instances involve products touted as containing certain proportions of post-consumer recycled material, yet lacking any confirmatory evidence. In essence, any claim featuring percentages or statistical data that isn't backed by credible verification is deemed unfounded
Sin of vagueness	It is defined by a vague statement, excessively generalized, and lacking precision, leaving its true significance susceptible to consumer misunderstanding	Labeling a product as "all-natural" illustrates this pitfall. Elements like arsenic, uranium, mercury, and formaldehyde are all naturally occurring yet toxic. The term "all-natural" does not inherently imply ecological responsibility
Sin of worshiping false labels	It is represented by a product that deceptively persuades consumers of its legitimate eco-certification through fraudulent labels or images	Examples may include meaningless phrases like "eco-reliable," which are used to present the product in a way that confuses the consumer

(continued)

Table 6.2 (continued)

Sins	Description	Example
Sin of irrelevance	It is identified by an environmental statement that may be accurate but is either irrelevant or provides no meaningful guidance to those in pursuit of greener alternatives	In this case, the label "CFC-Free"[1] serves as a common example, misleading consumers who often do not know that CFCs are legally banned in many countries
Sin of lesser of two evils	It is highlighted by an assertion that could be valid within its product class but potentially diverts consumer attention from the more significant environmental ramifications of the category at large	In this scenario, high-energy-efficient sports vehicles could serve as an example
Sin of fibbing	It is exemplified by deceptive eco-friendly claims	In this case, examples may include products that falsely claim to have attained environmental certification without actually having done so

Source Adapted from TerraChoice (2010)

crowdfunding campaigns where a company might launch a campaign aimed at financing a circularity project to divert attention from its actual unsustainable practices.

6.3 THE DIMENSION OF GREENWASHING IN REWARD-BASED CAMPAIGNS

In traditional markets, the advent of information technology has introduced new social media tools, allowing stakeholders to engage in novel forms of interaction and information sharing via the internet. Corporate websites and blogs, especially social media platforms such as Twitter and

---

[1] CFCs are chemical compounds containing chlorine, fluorine, and carbon. Attributed with causing the depletion of the ozone layer in the stratosphere, these substances have been prohibited under international accords, most notably the Montreal Protocol of 1987. As for Italy, the law enacted on June 16, 1997, set December 31, 2008, as the deadline for the production, utilization, marketing, importation, and exportation of CFCs.

132   F. CORSINI AND M. FREY

Table 6.3   Forms of corporate greenwashing implementation

Type of Practice	Description
Dirty Business	This variant of greenwashing emerges when companies, whose core activities are fundamentally unsustainable, tout sustainable practices or products that are neither emblematic of their overall operations nor reflective of the company's true character
Exaggerated Advertising	This form of greenwashing manifests in companies that divert attention from environmental sustainability issues through advertising. Specifically, such behavior is executed by sponsoring alternative programs unrelated to the most crucial and relevant environmental sustainability themes
Political Manipulation	This form of greenwashing materializes by influencing regulatory bodies or governments to gain benefits at the expense of environmental sustainability. These manipulations are often justified by the companies that employ them, claiming that they are major contributors or employers
It's the Law!	This form of greenwashing occurs by advertising compliance with laws and regulations as significant corporate achievements in sustainability
Obscure Reporting	This form of greenwashing manifests through the publication of sustainability reports where the implemented practices are ambiguously described, with the aim of distorting the truth or projecting a positive image in terms of Corporate Social Responsibility practices

Source Adapted from Contreras-Pacheco and Claasen (2017)

Facebook, are reshaping the dialogue and relationships between enterprises and their stakeholders. Within this milieu, the greenwashing risks intensify.

The practice of greenwashing has been growing to epidemic proportions in recent decades (Pimonenko et al., 2020), and this escalation is linked to a burgeoning trust issue, as consumers find it difficult to discern truthful claims (Nyilasy et al., 2014).

According to current research, the phenomenon's spread in crowdfunding appears sadly to be quite extensive. Already in Chapter 4, it was highlighted that an analysis of all projects aimed at creating circular products from 2009 to 2020 on the two major crowdfunding platforms suggested that nearly a third of the projects lacked detailed characteristics in introducing the projects, opting instead for generic terms like "sustainable" or "ecological."

This trend is unfortunately corroborated by other studies aiming to scrutinize the descriptive texts of some crowdfunding campaigns oriented toward developing sustainable and/or circular products (Champagne & Gianfrate, 2020). Specifically, the authors employ an evaluative grid based on objective criteria to closely examine the presentation texts of 219 reward-based crowdfunding projects. The study's findings reveal that only 27% of the campaigns present a low risk of greenwashing. Conversely, 46% of the campaigns are at medium risk. This group comprises a wide array of products (e.g., electric bicycles, air purifiers). These projects make some environmental claims, yet lack robust data to support such assertions. Moreover, according to the study's results, 22% of projects carry a high risk of greenwashing. Such projects spotlight an environmental claim unsupported by reliable information; many of these designate a product as "sustainable" based solely on one aspect (like energy savings) without considering other product features such as materials or end-of-life management. Some instances portray their project as a solution to a larger issue without explaining how it actually contributes to resolving that problem. Lastly, the research identifies a mere 4.6% of projects at high risk of greenwashing; most of these, in reality, have no sustainable features but employ many generic words and terms, likely to attract investors.

Completing the overview on the prevalence of the greenwashing phenomenon is the perception of those who have initiated a project—be they companies or private individuals who have launched a crowdfunding campaign. The authors of this volume have gathered this information through a questionnaire administered to more than 1,400 subjects who initiated a crowdfunding project related to the development of a sustainable or circular product.

The questionnaire was divided into various sections; the first aimed to collect information about the crowdfunding campaign. Specifically, in this section, we asked respondents about the platform where the project was published, the amount requested in the campaign, the amount received, the year of the campaign, the number of backers, and the type of sustainable products proposed. Another section aimed to gather the respondents' perceptions regarding the greenwashing practices of competitor companies and the level of agreement with potential initiatives that crowdfunding platforms could implement to curb greenwashing.

The questionnaire was distributed via email between November 2021 and March 2022, and the responses were collected on an online data collection platform. Out of 113 received responses, 76 referred to campaigns hosted on Kickstarter (76.26%), 26 to campaigns hosted on Indiegogo (23.01%), and the remaining 11 to campaigns hosted on both platforms (9.73%).

Figure 6.3 illustrates the perception of the greenwashing phenomenon among the 113 companies and/or individuals who have launched a crowdfunding campaign to develop a sustainable or circular product. As evident from Fig. 6.3, approximately 35% of survey participants agree with the proposed statement. Less than 10% disagree, and about 55% of respondents are uncertain.

This outcome highlights considerable uncertainty among the participants regarding the greenwashing phenomenon in crowdfunding campaigns; over a third expressed this uncertainty. Such ambivalence could reflect the difficulty in distinguishing between proper communication practices and those that resort to greenwashing. However, more than a third of respondents seem to have genuinely perceived instances of dishonest communication from competitors that may have impacted the success of their own product.

Further insights into the perception of the phenomenon can be gained by segmenting the 113 respondents based on the two crowdfunding platforms used to promote their projects, thereby understanding whether the perception of greenwashing is greater on Indiegogo or on Kickstarter. The results are presented in the following figure. Campaign promoters

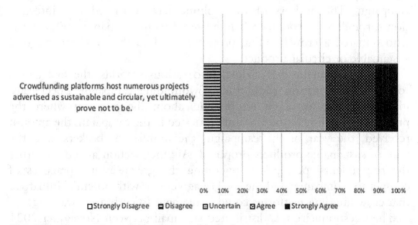

Fig. 6.3 Perception of the greenwashing phenomenon (*Source* Authors' elaboration)

who have used the Kickstarter platform are largely more uncertain about the phenomenon, with approximately 60% of the respondents falling into this category. In contrast, those who have used the Indiegogo platform appear to have a more clearly defined perception (Fig. 6.4).

The supplementary queries directed at the respondents sought to probe further into their understanding of the potential role that platforms might assume in curtailing greenwashing. Indeed, crowdfunding platforms could have a significant role in addressing the phenomenon of greenwashing by implementing initiatives designed to ensure the authenticity of sustainable campaigns. The adoption of such measures could enhance user trust in crowdfunding campaigns and foster the development of genuinely sustainable and circular solutions.

In this instance as well, the garnered replies are depicted in Fig. 6.5. As evident from the figure, the percentage of uncertain respondents drops considerably. In both instances, over 55% of the respondents agree with the development of standardized procedures and certifications to verify the actual sustainability of projects and their associated claims. This result indicates strong interest from the project proponents themselves in

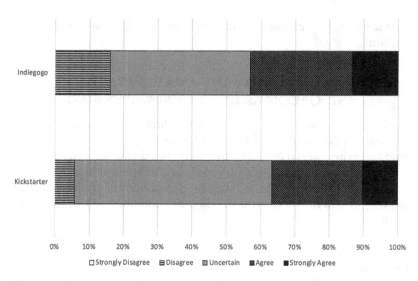

Fig. 6.4 Perception of greenwashing on major reward-based crowdfunding platforms (*Source* Authors' elaboration)

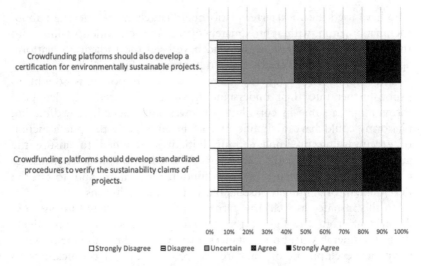

Fig. 6.5 The role of platforms in limiting the phenomenon of greenwashing (*Source* Authors' elaboration)

enhancing the transparency and reliability of campaigns on crowdfunding platforms.

6.4 How to Discourage Fraud and Greenwashing in Crowdfunding

As the chapter illustrates, while crowdfunding for sustainability offers promise as a democratic tool that enables the realization of projects with positive environmental impacts, navigating its risks and ethical challenges is essential for a successful path forward. In this sense, ethical considerations are not merely peripheral concerns; they are central to the credibility and long-term viability of crowdfunding as a tool for environmental and social change.

The potential risks associated with crowdfunding in the sustainability sector are numerous. These include the possibility of projects that are intentionally deceptive or fundamentally flawed in their environmental claims. The impact of such projects extends beyond individual backers, potentially discrediting the crowdfunding model itself and deterring future investment in genuinely sustainable initiatives. Moreover, the rapid growth of this sector could outpace existing regulatory frameworks, creating gaps that unscrupulous entities might exploit. Therefore, mechanisms to mitigate potential fraud are essential.

Firstly, it's crucial to emphasize the fundamental role that crowdfunding platforms must play in preventing fraud, particularly greenwashing. These platforms should take responsibility for verifying and validating companies' environmental claims seeking funding through their channels. This could involve forming a dedicated team of environmental experts to scrutinize each project closely. Implementing stringent verification processes could help ensure that only genuinely sustainable companies can present their ideas to investors as such. Moreover, crowdfunding platforms might collaborate with third-party organizations offering environmental certifications. Such organizations can provide an additional layer of verification and authentication for companies claiming to be green. Earning certification from an authorized body undoubtedly boosts investor confidence in a company's sustainability.

Additionally, given that some project proponents might unintentionally engage in greenwashing due to unfamiliarity with environmental issues, a possible tool could be an algorithm that provides a greenwashing risk score to creators while drafting their project descriptions (Champagne & Gianfrate, 2020). The algorithm could flag environmental claims and automatically request further supporting information for the statements made by the campaign's creator. Moreover, the algorithm could estimate features of greenwashing, like the use of vague terms such as "sustainable," "circular," and also the natural images used, alerting the campaign creator of potential greenwashing.

Regarding fraud and specifically greenwashing, educating investors is also vital. Greenwashing primarily targets investors who lack the means to verify environmental claims made by entrepreneurs. Here again, the role of crowdfunding platforms in educating investors is highly significant. For instance, platforms could offer educational resources, like guides or webinars, to help investors understand what truly constitutes a sustainable company and common greenwashing practices. Investors should also be encouraged to conduct their own research into the ventures they're considering funding and scrutinize company documents to validate claims.

Regulation is another key element in combating greenwashing; although various initiatives exist globally, increased stringency could be pivotal.[2] Regulatory authorities should introduce stricter rules on the transparency of environmental claims in the crowdfunding process. At the same time, penalties for false or misleading statements must be severe to discourage companies from attempting to deceive investors.

Lastly, media involvement and public opinion can also serve as potent deterrents against fraud and specifically greenwashing. Companies exposed for misleading environmental claims could suffer reputational damage, negatively affecting their crowdfunding success.

By combining these various approaches—stringent platform verification, investor education, regulation, and public pressure—it may be possible to create an environment where fraud and greenwashing in crowdfunding become increasingly challenging and unattractive for companies.

REFERENCES

Baum, L. M. (2012). It's not easy being green… or is it? A content analysis of environmental claims in magazine advertisements from the United States and United Kingdom. *Environmental Communication: A Journal of Nature and Culture, 6*(4), 423–440.

Belavina, E., Marinesi, S., & Tsoukalas, G. (2020). Rethinking crowdfunding platform design: Mechanisms to deter misconduct and improve efficiency. *Management Science, 66*(11), 4980–4997.

Champagne, M. L., & Gianfrate, P. G. (2020). *Exploring greenwashing on crowdfunding platforms.* Available at: https://www.afte.com/sites/default/files/inline-files/Mémoire%20du%203e%20prix%20ax%20aequo%20-%20Champagne%20Laetitia.pdf. Accessed on 1 December 2023.

Contreras-Pacheco, O. E., & Claasen, C. (2017). Fuzzy reporting as a way for a company to greenwash: Perspectives from the Colombian reality. *Problems and Perspectives in Management, 15*(2), 525–535.

Cumming, D., Hornuf, L., Karami, M., & Schweizer, D. (2021). Disentangling crowdfunding from fraudfunding. *Journal of Business Ethics, 182*(2), 1–26.

Delmas, M. A., & Burbano, V. C. (2011). The drivers of greenwashing. *California Management Review, 54*(1), 64–87.

---

[2] In March of 2023, the European Commission instituted a proposal for a Green Claims Directive. This initiative acts in tandem with, and puts into practical terms, the proposed directive centered on equipping consumers for the green transition. The directive's aim is to guarantee that consumers are furnished with trustworthy, comparable, and corroborated environmental data concerning products.

Federal Reserve. (2023). *Delinquency rates.* https://www.federalreserve.gov/rel eases/chargeoff/delallsa.htm. Accessed 12 April 2023.

Gatti, L., Seele, P., & Rademacher, L. (2019). Grey zone in–greenwash out: A review of greenwashing research and implications for the voluntary-mandatory transition of CSR. *International Journal of Corporate Social Responsibility, 4*(1), 1–15.

Hainz, C. (2018). Fraudulent behavior by entrepreneurs and borrowers. In *The economics of crowdfunding: Startups, portals and investor behavior* (pp. 79–99).

Ho, H. C., Chiu, C. L., Mansumitrchai, S., Yuan, Z., Zhao, N., & Zou, J. (2021). The influence of signals on donation crowdfunding campaign success during COVID-19 crisis. *International Journal of Environmental Research and Public Health, 18*(14), 7715.

Hornuf, L., & Schmitt, M. (2016). *Success and failure in equity crowdfunding.* CESifo DICE Report, 14(2), 16–22.

Hornuf, L., & Schwienbacher, A. (2016). Crowdinvesting: Angel investing for the masses? In *Handbook of research on business angels* (pp. 381–398).

Iyer, R., Khwaja, A. I., Luttmer, E. F., & Shue, K. (2015). Screening peers softly: Inferring the quality of small borrowers. *Management Science, 62*, 1554–1577.

Miramir. (2017). *Miramir—New social ecosystem for change.* Kickstarter. Retrieved May 7, 2024, from https://www.kickstarter.com/projects/maxsid orov/miramir-social-network-for-change

Mollick, E. (2014). The dynamics of crowdfunding: An exploratory study. *Journal of Business Venturing, 29*(1), 1–16.

Nielsen Media Research. (2015). *The sustainability imperative.* https://nielse niq.com/global/en/insights/analysis/2015/the-sustainability-imperative-2/. Accessed 15 April 2023.

Nyilasy, G., Gangadharbatla, H., & Paladino, A. (2014). Perceived greenwashing: The interactive effects of green advertising and corporate environmental performance on consumer reactions. *Journal of Business Ethics, 125*, 693–707.

Perez, B., Machado, S., Andrews, J., & Kourtellis, N. (2022). I call BS: Fraud detection in crowdfunding campaigns. In *Proceedings of the 14th ACM Web Science Conference 2022* (pp. 1–11).

Pimonenko, T., Bilan, Y., Horák, J., Starchenko, L., & Gajda, W. (2020). Green brand of companies and greenwashing under sustainable development goals. *Sustainability, 12*(4), 1679.

Santos, C., Coelho, A., & Marques, A. (2023). A systematic literature review on greenwashing and its relationship to stakeholders: State of art and future research agenda. *Management Review Quarterly, 74*(7), 1–25.

Signori, A., & Vismara, S. (2016). *Returns on investments in equity crowdfunding.* SSRN, 2765488.

Solar Roadways. (2014). *Solar Roadways. Indiegogo.* Retrieved May 7, 2024, from https://www.indiegogo.com/projects/solar-roadways

Tateishi, E. (2018). Craving gains and claiming "green" by cutting greens? An exploratory analysis of greenfield housing developments in Iskandar Malaysia. *Journal of Urban Affairs, 40*(3), 370–393.

TerraChoice. (2010). *The sins of greenwashing: Home and family edition.* http://sinsofgreenwashing.org/findings/the-seven-sins/. Accessed 11 April 2023.

Ziegler, Tania and Shneor, Rotem and Wenzlaff, Karsten and Suresh, Krishnamurthy and Paes, Felipe Ferri de Camargo and Mammadova, Leyla and Wanga, Charles and Kekre, Neha and Mutinda, Stanley and Wang, Britney and Closs, Cecilia López and Zhang, Bryan Zheng and Forbes, Hannah and soki, erika and Alam, Nafis and Knaup, Chris, The 2nd Global Alternative Finance Market Benchmarking Report (June 30, 2021). Cambridge, UK: Cambridge Centre for Alternative Finance. Available at SSRN: https://ssrn.com/abstract=3878065. Accessed on 29 September 2023.

CHAPTER 7

Crowdfunding and Proactive Environmental Strategies in the Organizational Life Cycle

Abstract In some instances, a crowdfunding campaign marks the inception of an entrepreneurial journey; in others, it is launched during periods of business growth or maturity to explore the creation of a new product or to secure funding for a new venture. This chapter aims to analyze crowdfunding in the context of an organization's life cycle. From the standpoint of environmental sustainability, a crowdfunding campaign may either be a preliminary experiment in an organization's project planning or be part of an already well-established trajectory. In this context, it becomes pertinent to understand the initiatives the organization has undertaken. Specifically, the chapter presents and discusses the results of a survey conducted among companies that have launched reward-based crowdfunding campaigns to understand what circular strategies they have adopted. The responses gathered from the survey reveal that for both existing companies that have employed crowdfunding in their business strategy, and those founded following a crowdfunding campaign, sustainability issues serve as a distinguishing feature rather than a fleeting interest.

Keywords Organizational life cycle stages · Funding strategies · Inception · Growth · Maturity environmental certifications

© The Author(s), under exclusive license to Springer Nature Switzerland AG 2024
F. Corsini and M. Frey, *Crowdfunding for Environmental Sustainability and the Circular Economy*,
https://doi.org/10.1007/978-3-031-66211-9_7

141

7.1 Crowdfunding in the Organizational Life Cycle

Crowdfunding, as a tool enabling the crowdsourcing of funds for project execution, can be used at various stages of a business life cycle. Some companies develop their entrepreneurial idea through a crowdfunding campaign and subsequently build a fully fledged enterprise based on that initiative. Others may launch a crowdfunding campaign during a phase of growth for an already established company to test a new product (e.g., through a reward-oriented crowdfunding campaign) or to raise funds for specific projects (e.g., through an equity crowdfunding campaign).

It should also be noted that there are crowdfunding projects that are not initiated by enterprises, and that may not result in the formation of a business post-campaign. For instance, a significant portion of projects developed through donation-based crowdfunding could fall into this category. Some reward-based crowdfunding initiatives might also be launched by individuals purely as amateur endeavors and do not lead to any form of entrepreneurial activity.

The theory of the organizational life cycle can help explain a company's motivation in launching a crowdfunding campaign by paralleling the characteristics of organizations at different phases of their evolution (Miller & Friesen, 1984). The model proposed by Miller and Friesen (1984) suggests that companies evolve through stages of birth, growth, maturity, decline, and revitalization (Fig. 7.1). The subsequent sections discuss these various life stages and how crowdfunding may be employed during them.

The inception of a company serves as a pivotal juncture in the organization's life cycle. During this phase, entrepreneurs ardently engage in defining and implementing the company's vision and mission. Not merely reliant on a robust business idea, this phase demands strategic planning acumen to transmute the idea into tangible reality. Characterized by high levels of enthusiasm, energy, and motivation among entrepreneurs, this stage necessitates a deep-rooted sense of identification and drive to surmount the myriad challenges that inevitably arise. The organizational climate is dynamic and inventive, fostering rapid ideation, testing, and implementation. Decisions are made swiftly, and the organization tends to be flexible, adapting to changes. Formalization of procedures is minimal

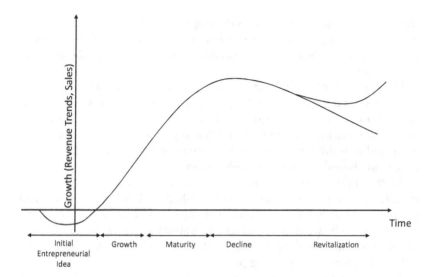

Fig. 7.1 Organizational life cycle (*Source* Adapted from Barringer & Ireland, 2010)

at this stage, allowing for fluid organizational structures that enable experimentation and innovation. However, as the enterprise survives and scales, formalization becomes increasingly inevitable.

Certain companies are born in the wake of a successful crowdfunding campaign, which, as discussed in Chapter 3, serves as a valuable tool for validating business ideas, garnering valuable feedback, and cultivating a supportive community. A successful crowdfunding campaign can be a positive indicator of future growth and success. However, the infancy of a company remains delicate; survival past this stage is not guaranteed. Mollick (2015) shows that around 8% of projects fail shortly after the campaign, failing even to deliver promised rewards.

The second life phase of a company is its development, which can be either rapid or gradual. Development may occur organically through business expansion or externally via outsourcing or strategic alliances. As the company grows, the workforce expands to meet increasing product or service demands, often requiring infrastructural enhancements. This period necessitates careful growth management to ensure that quality isn't compromised. Concurrently, profitability stabilizes as operational

144   F. CORSINI AND M. FREY

scale and efficiency increase. This developmental phase becomes a critical time where strategic and operational decisions can profoundly influence the company's long-term success, presenting both challenges and opportunities.

During a company's growth phase, crowdfunding can furnish the requisite capital for operational expansion, new product or service development, or market entry. Additionally, it can serve as a potent marketing platform, enhancing visibility and attracting new customers. Indeed, a successful crowdfunding campaign can catalyze significant media interest, potentially boosting sales and market share.

In the maturity phase, a company reaches its peak financial performance. Though stable and well-established, the vibrant energy and dynamism of earlier phases wane. This can be both a boon, indicating stability, and a bane, implying a lack of creativity and an appetite for innovation. Organizational rigidity can stifle adaptability, potentially eroding staff motivation and impacting productivity.

Once a company reaches maturity, it typically commands a stable market position with consistent products or services. However, unique challenges arise, such as the need for continual innovation and client engagement. Crowdfunding can play a pivotal role in overcoming these hurdles, offering capital for innovation and renewal. Direct customer engagement can foster loyalty and align innovations with customer needs.

Finally, the decline phase marks a terminal stage, characterized by deteriorating financial indicators. Faced with fierce competition or changing consumer behaviors, companies may experience a decline in clientele, directly affecting revenue and profitability. This can result in a crisis of confidence within the organization, leading to higher staff turnover and a loss of key talent. The decline phase demands decisive interventions to revitalize the company, offering the possibility of reverting to a trajectory of growth and success.

7.2   Proactive Environmental Strategies in Organizational Life Cycle

The theory of the organizational life cycle can indeed shed light on a company's inclination to adopt a proactive environmental strategy and focus on circularity. Literature on this subject reveals that businesses are most innovative during their phases of inception, growth, and revitalization. In contrast, the maturity and decline phases are generally more conservative (Adizes, 2004). Although each phase is distinct, an interplay of various complementary variables—such as situational, structural, and decisional factors—shapes the stages of the organizational life cycle, thereby influencing the degree of innovativeness and the adoption of proactive environmental and circular strategies.

Specifically, Adizes (2004) suggests that managerial attitudes during the phases of inception, growth, and revitalization are conducive to a high level of innovativeness and proactive behavior within the organization. On the other hand, companies in their maturity and decline phases typically exhibit a more conservative and reactive approach. This observation is supported by research related to the adoption of proactive environmental strategies (Primc & Čater, 2016) as well as circularity strategies (Primc et al., 2020). Particularly, in the stages of inception, growth, and revitalization, businesses often employ strongly proactive environmental strategies. To gain market share, companies at these stages might, for example, venture into competitive markets, thereby requiring an elevated degree of proactivity to adapt successfully to the changing industry landscape, seize new opportunities, and offer innovative solutions to market demand—often oriented toward distinctive features such as sustainable product development.

In the inception phase, adopting proactive environmental strategies can contribute to establishing a strong organizational identity, attracting sustainability-conscious investors, and achieving market differentiation. For instance, a company that decides to base its business model exclusively on the production of products using recycled materials instantly positions itself as a responsible and ecological entity. During the growth phase, proactive environmental strategies can further solidify the company's reputation, foster innovation, and attract an increasingly environmentally sensitive clientele.

In contrast, businesses in the more cautious phases of the organizational life cycle, specifically during periods of maturity and decline, tend to adopt a more reactive stance. As an illustration, sustainability strategies during these stages may serve to maintain competitiveness, manage environmental risks, and meet various stakeholder expectations (e.g., customers, suppliers, local communities). At this juncture, the level of innovation tends to wane, and companies are often more focused on preserving their existing achievements (Lester & Parnell, 2008). Such institutions are structured in a hierarchical manner, lack flexibility, and are bureaucratic in nature, with leadership choices tending to be more

146   F. CORSINI AND M. FREY

cautious and risk-averse rather than proactive (Miller & Friesen, 1984). Within such an organizational framework and modus operandi, taking a forward-thinking stance on environmental matters becomes a complex endeavor, necessitating a loosening of established norms and structures (Russo & Fouts, 1997). For firms in these more cautious life cycle stages, any alterations in external factors—be it shifts in consumer tastes or the rollout of new legislation—emerge as threats, given their restricted ability to adapt. As posited by Jawahar and McLaughlin (2001), true environmental foresight involves both anticipation and accountability and can only be set in motion if impending threats are recognized in advance. Should a threat already be present, the window for proactive measures has closed, leaving firms to craft reactive strategies to navigate the resulting changes. Assuming a proactive stance on environmental issues during these life cycle stages is intricate and calls for substantial shifts in value generation processes (Aragón-Correa & Sharma, 2003), engagement from a broad spectrum of stakeholders (Russo & Fouts, 1997), and concerted management dedication and orchestration (Aragón-Correa, 1998).

7.3   Questionnaire for Businesses that Have Conducted a Reward-Based Crowdfunding Campaign to Develop a Circular Product

The questionnaire elaborated in detail in Chapter 6 also included a section concerning the adoption of proactive environmental and circularity strategies. This was designed to gauge the interest of companies that have used crowdfunding in adopting such strategies during their organizational life cycle. Specifically, the questionnaire contained a question aimed at understanding at which stage of the organizational life cycle the companies had employed crowdfunding to develop a product adhering to circularity principles. The question sought to ascertain how many of the respondents were amateur endeavors versus established companies, and at what stage of the organizational life cycle they found themselves—offering options such as inception (the company was founded post-crowdfunding), growth, or maturity.

Of the 113 respondents who completed the questionnaire, 88 were companies that had utilized crowdfunding, while the remaining 25 responses came from individuals or groups who had initiated a campaign with the amateurish aim of bringing a product to life, but who did not operate within or on behalf of a company, or who had not found a company following their crowdfunding campaign. This outcome is not surprising, given one of the defining features of crowdfunding is its high accessibility. In this context, amateur initiatives can be launched by individuals or groups who may not have a formal business or professional background but are enthusiastic about an idea or a product and wish to bring it to fruition.

The remaining 88 companies, accounting for approximately 78% of the sample, were indeed established businesses. Table 7.1 illustrates the distribution of projects developed by these companies across three stages of the organizational life cycle: inception, growth, and maturity.

The questionnaire also included a section aimed at investigating the interest in implementing proactive environmental or circular strategies in the overall activities of the company, not just in relation to the product developed in the crowdfunding campaign. One of the circular strategies explored by the questionnaire pertained to adopting tools that support product design according to circular principles. This strategy signifies the company's intention to mitigate the environmental impact of its products, not just during the production phase, but throughout the product's entire life cycle. This includes considerations like using recycled materials, reducing water consumption in manufacturing, and extending the product's lifespan through design for durability or reparability (see Chapter 4). The use of guidelines or procedures for eco-friendly design suggests a systematic and coherent approach within the company.

Table 7.1 Number of companies responding to the questionnaire that were established immediately after a crowdfunding campaign (inception stage), in the growth phase, and in the maturity phase

Types of companies	Number	Percent(%)
Newly Established Companies Following a Crowdfunding Campaign (Inception Stage)	33	37.50
Companies That Have Used a Crowdfunding Campaign During the Growth Phase	22	25.00
Companies That Have Used a Crowdfunding Campaign During the Maturity Phase	33	37.50
Total	88	100

Source Authors' elaboration

148   F. CORSINI AND M. FREY

In circular design, significant emphasis is also placed on packaging design, which focuses on key areas such as reducing the packaging size, using recycled or recyclable materials, and designing mono-material packaging. In this context, adopting guidelines or procedures for eco-friendly packaging can substantially assist a company in lessening its environmental footprint.

The questionnaire further explored collaborations with other entities on issues related to circular economy. The goal of these partnerships could be to identify and implement actions and strategies that enhance the circularity of products and processes. Collaborations might involve universities and research centers, for instance through participation in joint research projects or contracts for accessing new technologies and manufacturing methods, up to sharing knowledge and expertise. Another form of collaboration can be established with other companies, potentially focusing on co-designing a product. Partnerships can also occur along the supply chain, such as working with suppliers to ensure the development of circular materials used in a product or its packaging.

Another aspect probed in the questionnaire is the adoption of a proactive communication strategy with customers to assist them in using products more responsibly and extending their lifespan. Providing usage information may include instructions on how to properly clean a product to maintain its condition and extend its longevity. For clothing items, specific instructions could be given on how to wash and dry them to avoid damage or wear. For products with rechargeable batteries, guidance on when and how to recharge could help prolong the batteries' lifespan. Finally, a company might offer information on repair, including details on how to obtain replacement parts or access repair services.

The last aspect scrutinized in the questionnaire relates to adopting a communicative approach that aids customers in making responsible decisions about product disposal at the end of its life. Providing end-of-life management information can include various aspects; the company might offer guidelines on how to properly recycle the product or its components. Some companies even offer product take-back programs at the end of a product's useful life. In this case, details on how to avail oneself of these programs could be provided.

To assess the level of adoption of the five circular strategies examined in the questionnaire, companies were asked to respond using a five-point Likert scale. Specifically, the available options for company responses were as follows: no, never; rarely; sometimes; most of the time; and always.

7.4 Comparison Among Companies that Have Utilized Crowdfunding in the Phases of Birth, Growth, and Maturity to Develop a Circular Product

In Fig. 7.2, responses from 33 startups are presented. As evident from Fig. 7.2, there is considerable interest among companies in employing guidelines for the sustainable design of all produced goods. Attention to the use of guidelines for designing all packaging is also evident, albeit slightly less than the former. Conversely, just over 5% of the 33 companies stated that they collaborate with other entities for the development of circularity projects; this aspect could potentially be attributed to the life cycle phase these companies currently find themselves in. From the gathered responses, it is also clear that there is high interest among companies in providing information on how to extend the useful life of the product, while slightly less interest exists among this group in offering insights on how to manage the end-of-life of their products.

In Fig. 7.3, responses from the 22 companies that have undertaken a crowdfunding campaign during their growth phase are showcased. As can be gleaned from Fig. 7.3, there is significant interest among these companies in utilizing guidelines for the sustainable design of their products—more than 80% of respondents claim to do this for all developed

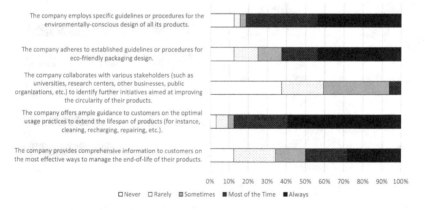

Fig. 7.2 Circular initiatives undertaken by newly established companies after the crowdfunding campaign (inception stage) (*Source* Authors' elaboration)

products. Interest in sustainable packaging design exists as well, although it is slightly less prevalent. Conversely, just over 5% of the 22 companies have indicated collaborating with other entities for the development of circular projects. From the gathered responses, it's evident that there is a high level of interest among these companies at this stage of their organizational life cycle in providing information on how to extend the useful life of their products. There is slightly less enthusiasm, however, in offering guidance on managing their products' end-of-life.

In Fig. 7.4, responses from 33 companies that have embarked on a crowdfunding campaign during their maturity phase are displayed. As evident from Fig. 7.4, there is a strong focus among these companies on adopting guidelines for sustainable product design, whereas interest in implementing guidelines for packaging design is less pronounced. Approximately 25% of the 33 companies claim to collaborate with external entities for the development of circular initiatives. The collected data reveals high enthusiasm among these companies in offering information on prolonging the useful life of their products, but marginally less interest in providing insights on managing the end-of-life of their products.

When comparing the two sets of figures—those related to companies in their inception phase and those in their growth phase—no notable differences arise. The interest in circular strategies across both stages appears to be significantly high. In this context, it can be concluded that the theme of circular economy, and more broadly, environmental

Fig. 7.3 Circular initiatives undertaken by companies in the growth phase (*Source* Authors' elaboration)

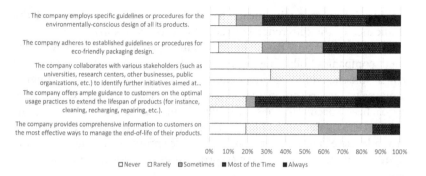

Fig. 7.4 Circular initiatives undertaken by companies in the maturity phase (*Source* Authors' elaboration)

sustainability, is not a fleeting choice linked solely to the crowdfunding campaign; rather, it characterizes all of their corporate decisions. A somewhat different scenario unfolds for businesses in their maturity phase. While these companies are fairly interested in adopting guidelines for sustainable product design and in providing information to extend their products' useful life, their interest is noticeably lower compared to the other two groups, as depicted in the figure below.

To discern if there are statistically meaningful variations in the adoption of circular strategies among firms that have incorporated crowdfunding into their business trajectory, including those founded post-crowdfunding campaigns, an Analysis of Variance (ANOVA) may be employed. This test is used to examine differences between sample means while considering their respective variances. The underlying principle of the test is to determine whether two or more sample means could come from populations that have the same parametric mean. For instance, the variance analysis could be employed to discern if there is a wage difference based on the type of degree among two or more groups of individuals. From the results of the variance analysis, we can ascertain if one of the group's mean is different from those of the other groups. Subsequently, a test can be used to compare pairs of means with equal variances, to identify which groups differ from each other. Although there are various types of tests that can be employed post-ANOVA (e.g., Bonferroni, Sidak, Scheffe, etc.), the Tukey test was used in this particular analysis.

Table 7.2 presents the means for the two reference groups and the significance of the difference between the recorded means.

The data emerging from the table illustrates that both newly established companies following a crowdfunding campaign and those in a growth phase exhibit greater interest in adopting circular strategies. Conversely, mature companies show substantially less interest in such approaches. Specifically, a statistically significant difference among the three groups is discernible concerning the intent to provide customers with adequate information on end-of-life product management and regarding the use of guidelines or procedures for eco-friendly packaging design.

The findings align perfectly with prior research on the subject, indicating that companies in their nascent and growth stages are more attentive to the adoption of proactive environmental strategies (Primc & Čater, 2016; Primc et al., 2020).

Additionally, the analyzed data suggest that proactive and circular environmental strategies characterize companies that have embarked on a crowdfunding campaign in their nascent and growth phases. On the other hand, companies in the maturity phase seem to abandon this interest, which could be attributed to various factors inherent to this stage of organizational development, such as resistance to change or the perception that implementing such strategies no longer offers profit benefits.

7.5 Environmental Certifications as a Sustainability Strategy

Among proactive environmental strategies is the option to secure environmental certifications for one's company or products. These certifications serve as a pivotal element in the realm of sustainability. Not only do they attest to an organization's commitment to sustainability, but they can also offer competitive advantages, as revealed by the questionnaire administered to companies that have launched a crowdfunding campaign. Specifically, the survey investigated the adoption rates of three types of certifications:

- Environmental Management Systems certification (e.g., ISO 14001);
- B-Corp certification;

Table 7.2 Adoption of circularity strategies in companies established immediately after a crowdfunding campaign (startup phase), in companies utilizing crowdfunding during the growth phase, and in those in the maturity phase

Circularity strategies investigated:	Newly established companies following a crowdfunding campaign (Inception stage)	Companies that have used a crowdfunding campaign during the growth phase	Companies that have used a crowdfunding campaign during the maturity phase	Comparison between pairs of averages with equal variances		
				Newly established companies vs. companies in the growth phase	Newly established companies vs. companies in the maturity phase	Companies in growth phase vs. companies in maturity phase
The company employs guidelines or procedures for the eco-friendly design of all its products	4.03	4.15	3.73	Difference Not Statistically Significant	Difference Not Statistically Significant	Difference Not Statistically Significant
The company adopts guidelines or procedures for the eco-friendly design of all packaging used	3.76	4.06	3.18	Difference Not Statistically Significant	Statistically significant difference with a p-value less than 0.1	Statistically significant difference with a p-value less than 0.05

(continued)

Table 7.2 (continued)

Circularity strategies investigated:	Newly established companies following a crowdfunding campaign (Inception stage)	Companies that have used a crowdfunding campaign during the growth phase	Companies that have used a crowdfunding campaign during the maturity phase	Comparison between pairs of averages with equal variances		
				Newly established companies vs. companies in the growth phase	Newly established companies vs. companies in the maturity phase	Companies in growth phase vs. companies in maturity phase
The company collaborates with other stakeholders (e.g., universities, research centers, other companies, public organizations, etc.) to identify additional actions aimed at improving product circularity	2.21	2.79	2.32	Difference Not Statistically Significant	Difference Not Statistically Significant	Difference Not Statistically Significant

Circularity strategies investigated:	Newly established companies following a crowdfunding campaign (Inception stage)	Companies that have used a crowdfunding campaign during the growth phase	Companies that have used a crowdfunding campaign during the maturity phase	Comparison between pairs of averages with equal variances		
				Newly established companies vs. companies in the growth phase	Newly established companies vs. companies in the maturity phase	Companies in growth phase vs. companies in maturity phase
The company provides customers with adequate information on the best ways to extend the lifespan of the products (e.g., cleaning, recharging, repairing, etc.)	4.39	4.06	3.91	Difference Not Statistically Significant	Statistically significant difference with a p-value less than 0.1	Difference Not Statistically Significant
The company provides customers with adequate information on the best ways to manage the end-of-life of the products	3.39	3.39	2.59	Difference Not Statistically Significant	Statistically significant difference with a p-value less than 0.05	Statistically significant difference with a p-value less than 0.05

Source Authors' elaboration

- Product certifications (e.g., Forest Stewardship Council, Ecolabel, Cradle to Cradle, etc.).

Subsequent sections briefly describe these certifications and then present and discuss the survey findings regarding companies that have conducted a crowdfunding campaign for the development of a sustainable and/or circular product.

Certified Environmental Management System (ISO 14001 and EMAS)

One primary type of environmental certification that companies can obtain focuses on verifying the adoption of an Environmental Management System (EMS). This system comprises the processes, procedures, tools, and models implemented by an organization, formalized to meet the requirements stipulated by reference standards such as ISO 14001 and the EMAS Regulation. Organizations that opt for certification make a tangible commitment to mitigating both their direct (resulting from their activities) and indirect (aspects they can influence) environmental impacts. The principal obligation of a certified organization lies in the continual improvement of its environmental performance. Thus, this certification serves as a process certification.

The initiation of the certification procedure begins with the establishment of an environmental management system, which the company can either execute autonomously or with the assistance of an external advisor. Once the system is in place, authorized bodies assess its conformity with the relevant legislation and grant the certification. Such certification must be renewed, for instance, every three years for ISO, through a designated renewal assessment, failing which it loses its validity.

The International Organization for Standardization (ISO) is among the most active entities in standardization and continuously develops management standards that address environmental concerns in organizations. Presently, it is working on crafting guidelines, supportive tools, and requirements for implementing circular economy strategies in businesses.[1] Among the most frequently employed ISO norms is the ISO

---

[1] ISO/TC 323 is the technical committee within ISO responsible for standardizing the practices and principles of the circular economy. The committee's progress can be tracked at the following link: https://www.iso.org/committee/7203984/x/catalogue/p/0/u/1/w/0/d/0.

14001 standard for environmental management systems, initially unveiled in 1996 and later revised in 2004 and 2015. ISO 14001 certification does not attest to a specific environmental performance but confirms that the certified organization possesses an adequate system for monitoring the environmental impacts of its activities, continuously seeking improvements in a coherent, effective, and above all, sustainable manner. ISO 14001 explicitly draws inspiration from the Plan-Do-Check-Act (PDCA) model, also known as the Deming cycle.

An alternative credential for environmental management systems is the Environmental Management and Audit Scheme (EMAS), formulated by the European Union. This instrument was crafted by the European Commission to empower businesses and various other entities to evaluate, disclose, and ameliorate their ecological performance. EMAS was initially introduced through Regulation No. 1836/93 and later amended by subsequent regulations, the most recent of which was issued at the end of 2009.[2] The primary objectives of this community regulation involve adopting an EMAS meeting the criteria set by UNI EN ISO 14001 to achieve continual improvement in a company's environmental performance and informing the public about the firm's environmental management via a document called the "Environmental Statement."

The B-Corp Certification

Another potential certification that businesses can adopt to demonstrate their commitment to sustainability issues is the B-Corp certification. Dissimilar to a particular statute, B-Corp certification offers a universal template that companies from any region or nation can adopt. The certification distinguishes enterprises that not only chase economic profits but also advance ecological and social sustainability.

The procedure for securing the certification unfolds across multiple phases. To begin with, an aspiring company completes a self-evaluative survey dubbed the Business Impact Assessment (BIA), which scrutinizes the firm's dedication in five key areas: human resources, governance, community involvement, ecological stewardship, and customer relations.

---

[2] Regulation (EC) No. 1221/2009 of the European Parliament and of the Council of November 25, 2009, on the voluntary participation of organizations in a Community eco-management and audit scheme (EMAS), repeals Regulation (EC) No. 761/2001 and Commission Decisions 2001/681/EC and 2006/193/EC.

Should the company garner a minimum score of 80 out of 200 in this preliminary assessment, they may advance to the verification stage, subjecting themselves to an audit conducted by the certifying body (B-Lab). Based on the documentation provided, B-Lab will decide whether to grant the certification or not.

To obtain certification, companies must also integrate their commitment to stakeholders into their statutory documents. In the United States, this can be accomplished through amendments to the charter or bylaws that explicitly state that stakeholder interests—such as employees, environment, suppliers, customers, local communities, and shareholders—will be considered. In various nations, the pathways for acquiring B-Corp certification differ; for example, in Italy, companies can fulfill the legal prerequisites for such certification by assuming the legal designation of a "società benefit," a concept introduced in the country in 2016.

Upon attaining the certification, firms are obligated to submit to regular appraisals of their conduct, maintaining a specified score range to retain their certified status. An annual financial contribution, fluctuating between $500 and $50,000 contingent upon the company's scale and earnings, is likewise mandated.

It's worth noting that B-Corp certification has received numerous criticisms in recent years (Diez-Busto et al., 2021; Fonseca et al., 2022; Liute & De Giacomo, 2022). Specifically, available documents do not provide clear and transparent criteria for when B-Lab performs a control visit, how that visit should be conducted, the competencies of the individuals performing the visit, or the criteria for awarding or denying B-Corp certification.

Product Certifications

Additional potential certifications that businesses can adopt to showcase their commitment to sustainability are product-based certifications. These allow companies to communicate their strategies and dedication to environmentally responsible production while enhancing the product's value.

One of the more well-known product certifications, particularly in European Union member states, is Ecolabel. It certifies various types of goods and services and was launched by the European Commission to enable consumers to identify products that meet high environmental standards. The certification endeavors to facilitate Europe's metamorphosis into a circular economy by examining the life stages of products—from the procurement of raw materials through to manufacturing, distribution, and eventual obsolescence.

Another esteemed product credential is Cradle to Cradle, applicable to an array of items such as apparel, construction materials, packaging, and furnishings. This certification gauges a product's circular sustainability across five dimensions: material composition, product recyclability, atmospheric and climate safeguards, water and land stewardship, and social fairness. Products are assigned a grade ranging from basic to platinum in each category, with the lowest score serving as the composite rating for the product.

Yet another instance is OEKO-TEX, specializing in textiles and fabrics. This entity provides six distinct certifications: Made in Green, Standard 100, Leather Standard, SteP, Responsible Business, and Eco Passport. Among these, Standard 100 enjoys the highest recognition and verifies that a product is devoid of over 100 deleterious substances.

The last example of product certification is the Forest Stewardship Council (FSC). This certification can be applied to wooden, paper, or wood-based products. FSC aims to establish standards for responsible forest management, such as supporting biodiversity protection, respecting local inhabitants' and workers' rights, and promoting environmentally sustainable forest management. Once certification is obtained, products can bear the FSC logo, assuring consumers that the wood or paper used comes from responsibly managed forests.

Interest in Environmental Certifications Among Companies that Have Conducted a Crowdfunding Campaign

To gauge companies' interest in the topic of certification, the survey provided respondents with the option to answer using a five-point Likert scale as follows: We are absolutely uninterested in such certification; We are currently not interested in such certification but will re-evaluate the possibility in the future; We are considering obtaining this certification; We are in the process of obtaining this certification; We have obtained the certification. The responses from the 88 companies are presented in Fig. 7.5.

Figure 7.5 reveals that companies which have undertaken a crowdfunding campaign to create a sustainable or circular product show scant interest in all three types of proposed certifications, especially those related

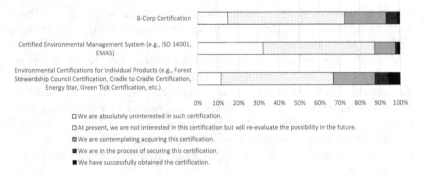

Fig. 7.5 Interest in certifications among companies promoting a crowdfunding campaign for the development of a sustainable product (*Source* Authors' elaboration)

to environmental management systems. This result may be ascribed to multiple influences, such as the belief that the certification procedure could be insufficiently recompensed by the marketplace.

Table 7.3 further presents responses broken down by the stage of the organization's life cycle. In this instance, although none of the differences between the groups are statistically significant, companies in the maturity phase report slightly lower interest in the certifications under consideration compared to companies in the inception and growth stages.

7.6 Conclusions

This chapter delineates crowdfunding within the life cycle of organizations and endeavors to elucidate the nexus between the phases of the life cycle and the adoption of proactive environmental and circular strategies.

The inclination of startups and burgeoning companies toward the adoption of such strategies underscores the emergence of a novel entrepreneurial awareness, oriented not solely toward economic triumph, but also toward positive environmental and social impact.

In this milieu, the presented findings unveil how crowdfunding can indeed serve as a conduit to experiment with and implement circular strategies from the nascent stages of a company's existence.

However, despite the manifested interest toward sustainability, environmental certifications seem to be greeted with lesser enthusiasm. This

7 CROWDFUNDING AND PROACTIVE ENVIRONMENTAL ... 161

Table 7.3 Adoption and interest in environmental certifications among companies formed immediately after a crowdfunding campaign (inception phase, growth phase, and maturity phase)

				Comparison between pairs of averages with equal variances		
Environmental certifications investigated:	*Newly established companies following a crowdfunding campaign (Inception stage)*	*Companies that have used a crowdfunding campaign during the growth phase*	*Companies that have used a crowdfunding campaign during the maturity phase*	*Newly established companies vs. companies in the growth phase*	*Newly established companies vs. companies in the maturity phase*	*Companies in growth phase vs. companies in maturity phase*
The company is interested in obtaining B-Corp Certification	2.39	2.24	2.05	Difference Not Statistically Significant	Difference Not Statistically Significant	Difference Not Statistically Significant
The company is interested in acquiring a Certified Environmental Management System	2.00	1.94	1.64	Difference Not Statistically Significant	Difference Not Statistically Significant	Difference Not Statistically Significant
The company is interested in securing Environmental Certifications for Individual Products	2.58	2.45	2.23	Difference Not Statistically Significant	Difference Not Statistically Significant	Difference Not Statistically Significant

Source Authors' elaboration

aspect may hint at a scant sensitivity on part of the campaign financiers toward these instruments, as well as among enterprises, underscoring the tangible benefits that can be gleaned in the corporate domain.

REFERENCES

Adizes, I. (2004). *Managing corporate lifecycles*. The Adizes Institute Publishing.

Aragón-Correa, J. A. (1998). Strategic proactivity and firm approach to the natural environment. *Academy of Management Journal, 41*(5), 556–567.

Aragón-Correa, J. A., & Sharma, S. (2003). A contingent resource-based view of proactive corporate environmental strategy. *Academy of Management Review, 28*(1), 71–88.

Barringer, B. R., & Ireland, R. D. (2010). *Successfully launching new ventures*. Pearson/Prentice Hall.

Diez-Busto, E., Sanchez-Ruiz, L., & Fernandez-Laviada, A. (2021). The B Corp movement: A systematic literature review. *Sustainability, 13*(5), 2508.

Fonseca, L., Silva, V., Sá, J. C., Lima, V., Santos, G., & Silva, R. (2022). B Corp versus ISO 9001 and 14001 certifications: Aligned, or alternative paths, towards sustainable development? *Corporate Social Responsibility and Environmental Management, 29*(3), 496–508.

Jawahar, I. M., & McLaughlin, G. L. (2001). Toward a descriptive stakeholder theory: An organizational life cycle approach. *Academy of Management Review, 26*(3), 397–414.

Lester, D. L., & Parnell, J. A. (2008). Firm size and environmental scanning pursuits across organizational life cycle stages. *Journal of Small Business and Enterprise Development, 15*(3), 540–554.

Liute, A., & De Giacomo, M. R. (2022). The environmental performance of UK-based B Corp companies: An analysis based on the triple bottom line approach. *Business Strategy and the Environment, 31*(3), 810–827.

Miller, D., & Friesen, P. H. (1984). A longitudinal study of the corporate life cycle. *Management Science, 30*(10), 1161–1183.

Mollick, E. R. (2015). Delivery rates on Kickstarter. *SSRN Electronic Journal*. https://doi.org/10.2139/ssrn.2699251

Primc, K., & Čater, T. (2016). The influence of organizational life cycle on environmental proactivity and competitive advantage: A dynamic capabilities view. *Organization & Environment, 29*(2), 212–230.

Primc, K., Kalar, B., Slabe-Erker, R., Dominko, M., & Ogorevc, M. (2020). Circular economy configuration indicators in organizational life cycle theory. *Ecological Indicators, 116*, 106532.

Russo, M. V., & Fouts, P. A. (1997). A resource-based perspective on corporate environmental performance and profitability. *Academy of Management Journal, 40*(3), 534–559.

CHAPTER 8

Conclusions

Abstract As discussed throughout the chapters of this volume, crowd-funding serves as a versatile tool to address the emerging challenges tied to sustainability and the transition toward a circular economy within enterprises. The essential premise is that businesses should not merely see crowdfunding as a fundraising mechanism, but as a multifaceted instrument capable of fostering collaborative product design between supply chain actors and, most importantly, end-users. The chapter suggests that crowdfunding can also be seen as a tool that facilitates feedback collection and garners comments, engenders a community of active supporters who believe in the company's values and its commitment to sustainability, and supports business model change.

Keywords Prosumerism · Co-design · Collaborative design · Circular materials · Circular business models · Product-as-a-service

8.1 Crowdfunding as an Enabler of Prosumerism

As examined in Chapter 4, design serves as a cornerstone in the circular economy. Here, the concept of design goes beyond the simple crafting of a product or service; it entails the involvement of the entire supply chain,

© The Author(s), under exclusive license to Springer Nature Switzerland AG 2024
F. Corsini and M. Frey, *Crowdfunding for Environmental Sustainability and the Circular Economy*,
https://doi.org/10.1007/978-3-031-66211-9_8

163

from material suppliers to end-users and waste management. This collaborative design approach, commonly known as co-design, is grounded in the collective sharing of knowledge between various supply chain actors, enabling the development of products and services that are easily reusable, repairable, and recyclable. Such stakeholders, when engaged in co-design activities, contribute their expertise on materials, construction methods, and other key aspects related to the product's life cycle.

This form of collaborative design can be facilitated and stimulated through crowdfunding. As presented in Chapter 4, crowdfunding offers the unique opportunity for not just investors but also consumers to actively participate in the ideation and development stages of the product. The latter can contribute their skills, ideas, and suggestions, influencing both design and implementation while ensuring that sustainability considerations are met. In this setting, the consumer effectively becomes a "prosumer," highlighting the active role consumers can assume in the creative processes of product conception and design. This new vision of prosumerism emphasizes not just consumption choices and habits but also the direct contribution that consumers can bring to product design through their knowledge and experience. Crowdfunding not only facilitates the creation of more sustainable and circular products through financial support but also encourages greater consumer responsibility and engagement, transforming consumers from mere end-users into active participants in the production process.

Considering the significance of co-design in advancing a transition to a circular economic system, it becomes increasingly vital to understand how to enhance consumer-business interaction. Undoubtedly, direct incentives are one of the most effective methods to engage consumers in co-design. Transforming consumers into prosumers, social motivators—those that operate at the interpersonal level and allow individuals to publicly support a company while addressing complex entrepreneurial challenges and achieving personal satisfaction—are found to be more impactful than tangible rewards (Ziemba & Eisenbardt, 2016).

In this context, a corporate strategy to further engage supporters in enhancing the product's environmental features could involve offering participation in the co-design of these aspects as a reward in a crowdfunding campaign. This approach has been identified as a best practice for funding innovative products (Thürridl & Kamleitner, 2016) and could be similarly effective for products focused on sustainability and circularity.

Another managerial recommendation could be to grant the campaign's most active supporter a position on the company's environmental advisory board, thereby acknowledging their knowledge contribution and providing additional benefits in the development of new products. This strategy would not only enhance customer engagement but also encourage them to provide constructive feedback and actively participate in product design. If reward-based crowdfunding serves as a mechanism to promote co-design for circularity, equity crowdfunding, conversely, can facilitate the research into circular materials. As noted in Chapter 4, design in the circular economy should also encompass the development of new circular materials, where equity crowdfunding could serve as a powerful facilitator.

Innovation in environmentally friendly materials primarily follows two paths: the first involves materials designed within the circular economy framework, constructed with circular principles from the start (Pellizzari & Genovesi, 2017). These materials are designed, developed, and disposed of either to be recycled or to minimize environmental impact. The second path includes materials aimed at enhancing the efficiency of other products, such as insulating materials for buildings (Pellizzari & Genovesi, 2017).

Research and experimentation with new materials are essential to accelerate the transition process, addressing the current challenges associated with using such materials. These challenges may include inconsistent availability, higher costs, or longer supply times compared to traditional materials. For example, materials sourced from industrial symbiosis[1] or production waste, which through innovative production processes and technologies can give rise to new materials and promising supply chains. In this scenario, equity crowdfunding can provide the necessary capital to develop new materials, enhance existing technologies, and transition ideas from the lab to the marketplace. Funds can be used for research and development, equipment purchase, infrastructure construction, and business expansion.

---

[1] Industrial symbiosis is a process where resources such as by-products, waste, or unused energy residues, as well as underutilized services from one company or industrial activity, become raw materials for another company or production process. This process aims to establish interdependent relationships where production waste, energy, and so forth circulate continuously, mirroring what occurs in natural ecosystems.

166   F. CORSINI AND M. FREY

Some equity crowdfunding campaigns are indeed aimed at developing sustainable materials, using, on one hand, plant fibers derived from agro-industrial waste and, on the other, materials like bioplastics suitable for various industrial technologies, such as extrusion and 3D printing.

8.2   CROWDFUNDING AS A TOOL FOR INITIATING NEW CIRCULAR BUSINESS MODELS

As noted in Chapter 2, economic barriers and a lack of funding are the primary hindrances faced by businesses in the transition to a circular model. Financing targeted projects to enhance production processes is challenging enough; financing a complete overhaul of a business model to adopt a more sustainable and circular one could be nearly prohibitive. For instance, circular business models involve creating value through the use of entirely renewable, recyclable, or biodegradable materials that can be employed in consecutive life cycles. Such models may also focus on product recovery and recycling or the incorporation of by-products into production circuits, often facilitated through industrial symbiosis agreements with other types of businesses, with the aim to reintroduce valuable materials, energy, and components into the production loop. Others extend the lifespan of a product, thereby mitigating the loss of value that occurs at the end of a product's life through repair, upgrades, and regeneration. Increasingly, business models are emerging that rely on sharing platforms to create commercial opportunities for both consumers and companies by facilitating the rental, sharing, or exchange of unused goods. Finally, the "product-as-a-service" model is a key element in transitioning toward a circular economy. This model allows producers to retain ownership and control over a product during its usage phase, offering the customer merely the utility or functional performance of the product. By maintaining ownership and focusing solely on performance, this model internalizes waste management costs and even incentivizes the reduction of resource consumption (Manzini & Vezzoli, 2003).

However, the adoption of such business models has been slow to date. Among numerous challenges, one key issue is financial. In a traditional sales model, revenue is realized at the end of the production cycle, whereas in a "product-as-a-service" model, revenue is generated over the product's useful life, potentially leading to liquidity issues for the business. In this context, crowdfunding can serve not only as a useful financial tool but also as a means for creating a community interested in the company's services. One exemplary case is that of the Dutch company Bundles, which offers high-quality appliances through subscription plans. The appliance is delivered and installed in the customer's home but remains the property of Bundles. Clients pay according to the selected subscription and usage cycles. Bundles manages delivery, installation, and maintenance while also providing additional services like detergent supply. The company successfully raised €500,000 through three equity crowdfunding campaigns hosted by the Dutch platform OnePlanetCrowd, thereby building a promotional community that includes some of its funders as customers.

In broader terms, considering the innovative and complex nature of circular business models (Bocken et al., 2018), crowdfunding can also allow businesses to refine their value propositions and distribution strategies.

8.3 Managerial Considerations for Conducting a Crowdfunding Campaign for Sustainability Projects

This volume also highlights some managerial implications for companies aiming to utilize crowdfunding to develop projects connected to environmental sustainability and circular economy. Specifically, Chapter 5 examines factors affecting crowdfunding success and offers insights for businesses. Success in crowdfunding requires meticulous strategic planning, including identification of the target audience, achievable financial goals, potential rewards, and effective communication strategies. All these factors significantly influence the success of the campaign across various crowdfunding types, such as donations, rewards, loans, and equity.

However, when the crowdfunding is aimed at a sustainability or circular economy project, there are additional aspects to consider. For instance, transparent communication about environmental and circular performance is essential to mitigate the risk of greenwashing. Companies should provide verified and authentic environmental data, possibly supported by third-party certifications. Crowdfunding serves not just as a fundraising tool but also as a means to build a community around the project and the company. Transparent communication and involving potential funders in design choices can enhance the bond with stakeholders and also yield insights into customer needs and desires.

Another managerial suggestion for companies interested in crowd-funding for sustainability projects is to collaborate with experts in the fields of sustainability and circular economy. Partnerships with non-governmental organizations focused on environmental goals can provide valuable insights to increase campaign credibility and reach a broader audience. Lastly, the use of certifications is currently underutilized in crowdfunding but could be an invaluable tool for reaching a wider audience and gaining a competitive advantage.

8.4 Role and Strategies of Platforms Specializing in Supporting Projects Generating Positive Environmental Impact

While traditional crowdfunding platforms have gained widespread prominence in recent years, there remains significant growth potential for platforms focused on supporting projects that yield a positive environmental impact. As discussed in Chapter 3, recent years have witnessed the emergence of specialized crowdfunding platforms that exclusively back projects committed to social initiatives and environmental sustainability (e.g., civic crowdfunding for environment-related projects, energy crowdfunding, etc.).

Within this context, crowdfunding can metamorphose into a variant of "impact investing"—capital allocations designed with the goal of yielding quantifiable social and environmental benefits, in addition to financial gains. Such impact-oriented investments can target either emerging or established markets and strive for a spectrum of returns, from subpar market yields to market-level rates, contingent on the investors' strategic aims (Troise et al., 2020).

For long-term success, specialized crowdfunding platforms must develop competitive strategies that distinguish them from traditional platforms, effectively reaching the investor market interested in generating additional environmental impact alongside financial returns. One such strategy should involve more rigorous due diligence processes for projects. This is imperative for ensuring that these platforms don't facilitate fraudulent behavior like greenwashing, a phenomenon highlighted in Chapter 6. Currently, many traditional crowdfunding platforms conduct minimal checks, thereby lowering the barriers to entry. Lax due diligence processes could encourage behaviors incompatible with the creation of meaningful social or environmental impact and could ultimately tarnish the crowdfunding market's reputation, eroding investor trust.

Another strategic lever for specialized crowdfunding platforms should be their capability to assist companies in forming partnerships and collaborations aimed at maximizing the projects' environmental impact (Picón Martínez et al., 2021). Specialized platforms could significantly enhance a project's positive impact by facilitating collaboration with other crowdfunding platforms and various types of investors (e.g., foundations, investment funds, and other financial institutions). Within this context, platforms might also assist companies in securing additional funding through other channels. Moreover, specialized crowdfunding platforms could offer support in forming partnerships capable of enhancing a project's impacts, for example, by facilitating relations with universities and research centers. Currently, as outlined in Chapter 6, such initiatives are not widely adopted by companies utilizing crowdfunding. Universities and research centers can offer technical and scientific expertise essential for a project's development and success. For instance, they could provide the necessary support to measure the positive environmental impacts accurately, thus allowing proper communication of the project's environmental performance.

The final strategic lever for equity and loan-based specialized crowdfunding platforms could be managing investors' exit strategies. In this regard, platforms might focus their efforts on the termination of investments, identifying potential subsequent investments related to sustainability that investors might find appealing.

References

Bocken, N. M., Schuit, C. S., & Kraaijenhagen, C. (2018). Experimenting with a circular business model: Lessons from eight cases. *Environmental Innovation and Societal Transitions, 28,* 79–95.

Cafferkey, P., Picón Martínez, A., & Gianoncelli, A. (2021). *Accelerating the SDGs—The role of crowdfunding in investing for impact.* EVPA.

Eisenbardt, M., & Ziemba, E. (2016). Incentives encouraging prosumers to knowledge sharing—Framework based on polish study. *Online Journal of Applied Knowledge Management, 4*(2), 146–166.

Genovesi, E., & Pellizzari, A. (2017). *Neomaterials in the circular economy.* Edizioni Ambiente.

Jones, P., Troise, C., & Tani, M. (2020). Investigating the impact of multidimensional social capital on equity crowdfunding performance. *International Journal of Information Management, 55,* 102230.

Kamleitner, B., & Thürridl, C. (2016). What goes around comes around? Rewards as strategic assets in crowdfunding. *California Management Review, 58*(2), 88–110.

Manzini, E., & Vezzoli, C. (2003). A strategic design approach to develop sustainable product service systems: Examples taken from the 'environmentally friendly innovation' Italian prize. *Journal of Cleaner Production, 11*(8), 851–857.

INDEX

A
Access to Financing, 31

B
Barriers to Circularity, 24
B-Corp Certification, 152
Blockchain, 7
Business Model Innovation, 4

C
Circular Economy, 3, 15, 163
Circular Economy Policies, 22
Circular Products, 70, 75
Crowdfunding Platforms, 43
Crowdfunding Projects, 74

D
Design for Circularity, 62, 69

E
Environmental Certifications, 152

Environmental Management System, 152
Equity Crowdfunding, 54

F
Fraud in Crowdfunding, 120

G
Greenwashing, 126

I
Industrial Ecology, 16
Internet of Things (IoT), 7
ISO 14001, 152

L
Linear Economy, 16
Loan-Based Crowdfunding, 51

© The Editor(s) (if applicable) and The Author(s), under exclusive
license to Springer Nature Switzerland AG 2024
F. Corsini and M. Frey, *Crowdfunding for Environmental Sustainability and the Circular Economy*,
https://doi.org/10.1007/978-3-031-66211-9

INDEX

P
Prosumers, 164

R
Reward-Based Crowdfunding, 49

S
Shared Value Creation, 5
Specialization in Crowdfunding
    Platforms, 56
Sustainable Development, 3, 21

V
Value Creation, 33